T0248265

"Dain Walker is the epitome of a branding virtuoso, seamlessly merging strategic prowess with an intuitive understanding of market dynamics. His unparalleled expertise has not only elevated brands to new heights but has also served as a beacon of inspiration for those fortunate enough to collaborate with him. Working alongside Dain has been an enlightening journey, where his keen insights and forward-thinking approach have reshaped my perspective on brand development. Without hesitation, I wholeheartedly recommend Dain to anyone seeking to establish a lasting and impactful presence in today's competitive landscape."

—Fred Schebesta, founder of Finder

"Dain is beyond a branding expert; he's a brand therapist. He was able to get inside my brain and extract the details about my brand that I didn't even know. He turned my abstract feelings into art and copy, and took me to the next level."

—Mark Gagnon, comedian, cost of Camp Gagnon, and cohost of Flagrant Podcast

THE
90 DAY
BRAND
PLAN

DAIN WALKER

THE 90 DAY BRAND PLAN

How to
**Unleash Your
Personal Brand**
to Dominate
the Competition
and Scale Your
Business

WILEY

Published by John Wiley & Sons, Inc., Hoboken, New Jersey.
Published simultaneously in Canada.

For general information on our other products and services or for technical support, please
contact our Customer Care Department within the United States at (800) 762-2974, outside
the United States at (317) 572-3993 or fax (317) 572-4002.

Wiley also publishes its books in a variety of electronic formats. Some content that appears
in print may not be available in electronic formats. For more information about Wiley
products, visit our web site at www.wiley.com.

Library of Congress Cataloging-in-Publication Data is available:

ISBN: 9781394221097 (cloth)
ISBN: 9781394221110 (ePub)
ISBN: 9781394221103 (ePDF)

Cover Design and Image: © Jared Wineera

SKY10070690_032624

Contents

Thank You

This book is dedicated to my wife, Elli Walker. Thank you for being my best friend, my partner in life, and for forever and always having my back no matter the venture I set out on—from sleeping on the floor in debt to growing a flourishing business together. You brighten my soul and I'm grateful for all that you do for me.

To my children, Harlo and Joey, who I hope will see the power of what happens when you give with an open heart, do good in the world, and create opportunities for others to chase their dreams. You both fill my heart with joy, keep me present, and remind me there are endless cherished moments together to be grateful for.

To Campbell Nugent and Denis Kucukovic for the late nights, early mornings, and tirelessly supporting me in my busy schedule to unpack my years of teachings and carefully articulate how I poured my mind into this book.

To Jared Wineera for supporting my vision for the agency Rivyl when it was merely an idea, for being an endearing friend pushing me to strive for more than I felt I deserved, for growing this group of wild creatives into a company we can forever be proud of, and for the beautiful illustrations you provided within this book.

Also, to Gary Vee, who inspired me to get off my ass and just fucking start.

And finally, to the team at Rivyl, for your constant devotion to our mission with your wildly creative ideas, the love and care you give to our clients, and how you constantly urge me to take ourselves to new heights.

Chapter 1

PERSONAL BRANDS FILL STANDS

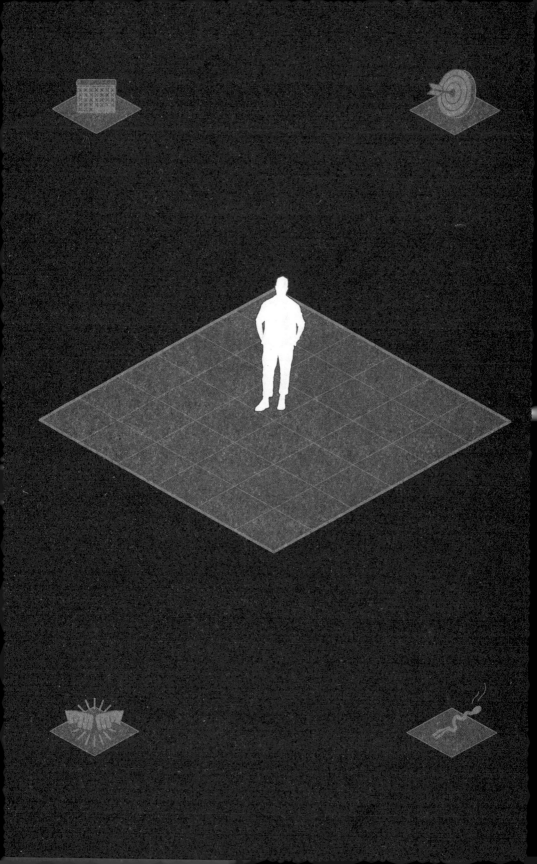

I stood in front of my company, exchanging gifts and bonuses at our annual end-of-year wrap-up, looking around at my team's faces. I found myself completely shaken by how far we had come in just three short years. Just four years prior, this was all an insane idea in my head, an idea I had while working my full-time retail job selling phones.

Before all of this, building a branding agency was purely a delusional and lofty "one day" goal of mine—something to dream about in the distant future. Back then I felt alone, afraid, yet I ventured into the unknown, with no guarantee of success, no money in my bank account, no previous business experience, no mentors or coaches—just stubbornness and the will to have a crack at something I had never done before: branding myself publicly. This is what I worked on for the next couple of years.

And what did I achieve after all this time? My agency Rivyl. A crew of 20 mavericks (an endearing term we use to refer to our team for their rebelliously creative nature), all responsible for an average of 70 client projects to juggle every month. They laughed, made fun of each other, and relished in the unfathomable success we had created for ourselves in such a short time frame as an aggressive start-up. They joked about their onboarding interviews in years past, when they'd initially questioned whether the company was a scam or not, questioned whether it would make it past the start-up phase or not. Starting in June 2022, Rivyl began hiring new employees every week and fitting out a new office in the heart of Sydney, Australia, north of the Harbour Bridge, with art and furnishings. My team applauded themselves for taking the plunge despite the initial risks. We celebrated the spoils of war together and plotted our course to climb to new heights in the following year.

Fast-forward to 2023. My team at Rivyl had just experienced unprecedented and admittedly unexpected success: completing a project that involved developing strategy and a complete brand design update for our client Simon Beard and his company Culture Kings, a $600 million global suburban fashion retailer. Rivyl had prepared them for their launch into the US market on the Las Vegas strip; and their new flagship store was located in the largest retail space in Caesar's Palace. The store fitout and preparation for the project were crazy! The store featured the world's largest hat wall (three stories tall), a secret VIP room with exclusive limited-edition Nike Air Jordan drops, a basketball court in the middle of their store, a DJ booth overlooking the outlet, and the crowning jewel: a recording studio in the middle of the store for their frequent celebrity appearances, such as Snoop Dog, Drake, A$AP Rocky, Juice WRLD, Justin Bieber, and more.

I'm writing this not to impress you, but to impress on you, that all of this happened because I built a personal brand.

My personal brand was the reason I made enough money to quit my job and work for myself. My personal brand was the reason I got my first client for my agency. My personal brand was the reason talent in my industry sought me out and demanded I let them work for me. My personal brand was the reason I was invited to share stages with life and business strategist Tony Robbins, author and business consultant Seth Godin, public speaker and educator Chris Do, entrepreneur Lewis Howes, sporting legend Tom Brady, business mogul Simon Beard, and businessman Tom Bilyeu. My personal brand was the reason I was able to build a multi-seven-figure company. My personal brand was the reason I had taken my company from a small start-up to 20+ employees in just three years. My personal brand was the reason I started Australia's fastest growing branding agency. My personal brand was how I landed the job with the CEO of Culture Kings and consulted with other brands such as CitiBank, Coca-Cola, JPMorgan Chase, and LSKD. My personal brand is the reason I'm writing this book; the publisher sought *me* out! All of this because I decided to build a personal brand when I was employed but in debt and wondering what I wanted to do with my life.

Having a personal brand gave me credibility in my industry. It gave me the altitude to position myself as a global expert and thought leader in all things branding. It prequalified me as a viable option to potential clients and companies because of my perceived value from my social validation.

Because of the prolific nature of my social media content, I became sought after as the solution for the branding problems I identified and frequently talked about. To my initial shock, CEOs and global brands (such as those that I just mentioned) sought out my expertise, because in their mind, I had all the answers. In their mind, I was the person who really could solve their branding problems. And I found a way to monetize this. The whole reason for this book is to show you how to do this yourself. As intimidating as this might sound, anyone can do their version of this with the right tools and frameworks—whatever that looks like to you.

I crafted a personal brand so that I could serve up opportunities for myself on a golden platter—not knowing what they would be on the out-look, but knowing they would arrive if I got my face out of obscurity and into the limelight.

It's crazy to think back now that I ever had doubts, but I did. It's weird to think that the unhelpful opinions from my colleagues at the start mattered, because now they don't. It's odd to think that, had I never taken the leap of faith to get uncomfortable and expose myself to ridi-cule, I would not be writing this for you right now. At that time it was difficult to imagine anyone working for me as a consultant, let alone 20+ mavericks. I never thought in my wildest dreams, having grown up wearing Culture Kings apparel, that my team and I would be redesigning their logo and consulting with them on how to photograph their models, how to optimize their e-commerce platform, or what fonts they should be using on their store signage. I never saw myself as someone valuable that CEOs and founders of billion-dollar companies would call for advice on their personal and corporate branding. But here I am, and if I can do it, you can do it!

Personal Branding Versus Company Branding

Do a favor for me. Whip out your phone and perform a quick social media search of the people in the following figure and their personal brands so that you can see how evident the impact of personal branding is. We care far more about people, their stories, their ideas, their actions, wins, losses, and behaviors than we care about corporations. People love people far more than they love companies.

Compare the number of followers each pair:

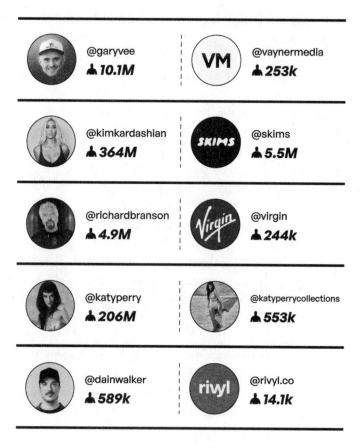

@garyvee 👤 10.1M	@vaynermedia 👤 253k
@kimkardashian 👤 364M	@skims 👤 5.5M
@richardbranson 👤 4.9M	@virgin 👤 244k
@katyperry 👤 206M	@katyperrycollections 👤 553k
@dainwalker 👤 589k	@rivyl.co 👤 14.1k

What's glaringly evident is that the gap between their personal branding and corporate branding is not only palpable—it's unmistakable. Each one of these personal brands has more followers, more engagement, and more organic reach on social platforms than their corporate brands do. There is a science to this, and it's that human beings are wired to connect to people, not objects. And that's a big reason for the surge of influencers in today's market.

According to *Fortune* magazine, "92% of consumers trust recommendations from friends over information delivered through traditional ads."[1]

The recent cultural buzzword and phenomena of the influencer—an individual who has the capability to alter the belief systems of people—fits this statistic perfectly. The term *influencer* isn't even a modern one—it's existed since the 1600s,[2] but its definition was expanded when it became a way to label the social media phenomenon of people leading others into buying things and joining causes they endorsed. This is not a new concept though; we humans have been doing this as far back as our records go. We want to wear the clothes celebrities wear, we want to drive the cars our friends drive, we want to listen to the music our friends listen to. We see movies our colleagues suggest we see, we hit that eating spot our family tells us is "to die for." And this is why marketing heads and salespeople suggest taking advantage of influencer culture, because it stands to be a modern monetization technique.

This has been the case for years. As a matter of fact, *Forbes* tells us that "in 2012, 78.6% of sales people using social media to sell out-performed those who weren't using social media."[3]

When consultants, coaches, representatives, and reps work to impress us, we ask ourselves, "Are they worth listening to? What makes them an expert? Can they be trusted?" If we find that their social media is popping off with tens of thousands of followers, then in our minds . . . they have altitude. They have social proof that they're a high-networked individual who's highly sought after, with advice we should trust. Social media is the business card of the modern age. For our parents, it was a job title. For us, it's about how many people follow this person.

In the United States, according to *Harvard Business Review*, "70% of employers check out applicants' profiles as part of their screening process, and 54% have rejected applicants because of what they found."[4]

Even when you're looking for a new job, you're not safe from the grip of your personal brand. I dare you to ask your most recent boss if they looked at your socials before hiring you. I'm almost certain they did. I admit that I do it. When people apply to Rivyl, I punch their name into Google and gain insights into what they care about, their opinions, what kind of person they are, and if they're a good cultural fit for my team or not. Your social media pages tell the world a lot about you—and if you don't have a social media following and rarely disclose anything, then that's also saying something. Some may see this as harsh, but given that at Rivyl, we're hiring for a job in *branding,* if a candidate doesn't have any social media presence, we don't hire them.

 Make Your Mark

Whether we're aware of it or not, we all have a personal brand. If we're not using it to leverage opportunities in business, we're using it to keep our friends posted on what we had for breakfast, or we tag where we spent our holidays and take photos with our families. We share our opinions online, we debate with people, we comment on things. You can even gain a lot of information about someone by looking at whom they follow. Many broadcast their political beliefs. We even say a lot by what clothes we wear and how we take photos. We write bios about ourselves informing people about what we do, where we work, and what we care about. If you're reading this, I'm assuming you've engaged with social media in some shape or form. My question to you, however, is whether you're using it to its full advantage to get more opportunities in life like it has for me.

In my experience, the majority of my social media engagement activity has been with people asking me for advice. And that has been the major reason for my success in my industry.

What anyone with a cadence in sales, marketing, and advertising would see here is "money." I asked myself, "If people are using social platforms as a means of consulting, problem-solving, insight-seeking, consumer recommendations, advice, tips, and direction, then, how can I leverage it?" To that, my answer was personal branding! I learned to use my public profile as a means to direct attention and traffic toward the things that would enable me to grow Rivyl by carefully and creatively promoting my products, services, events, and companies. I used personal branding as a free mechanism to alter the belief systems of people. I used my personal brand to educate business owners on the power of branding—and how, by participating in services with myself, they could get what they wanted (the ability to scale their companies) and do for themselves what I do for myself.

This is how you do what you've always wanted. Something great.

Jeff Bezos: He launched the first version of Amazon Prime at the end of 2004, then officially announced it to the public six weeks later in February 2005. The motto for Amazon Prime was "Shipping in 6 weeks or less. Guaranteed." Now, it's way quicker.[5]

Jessica Alba: Her "Honors Company" rose to instant success, garnering over $10,000,000 in 2012, its first year of existence.[6]

Tony Fadell: He led the infamous iPod project in 2001, pitching the concept to Steve Jobs in March. The first iPods shipped to adoring customers in November of the same year.[7]

Walt Disney: Disneyland ended up going from Walt Disney's mind to an actual reality in just 366 days. It's now known as "the happiest place on earth."[8]

Brendan Eich: He wrote the first prototype of JavaScript in May 1995 in only 10 days. He then shipped the beta four short months later.[9]

Brehon Somervell: He made the plans for the Pentagon building, the world's largest office building at the time, in just four days! The project began construction two months later and only took 491 days to complete.[10]

Sylvester Stallone: He wrote the screenplay for *Rocky* in three-and-a-half days. Principal photography on the film was completed in just 28 days, with a budget under $1,000,000.[11]

Napoleon Bonaparte: In just 100 days, between March and June 1815, he escaped from prison in Elba, gathered 600 fighting troops and landed with them at Cannes, recruited an entire regiment, marched with them to Paris to recapture the government, increased his army to a size of 280,000 troops, marched into and invaded Belgium, defeated the Prussians with half an army, finally lost to a combined army of Wellington and Anglo-Prussian forces at Waterloo, was removed from his throne, and ended up once again in prison, this time at St. Helena.[12]

 # Do It in 90 Days

Human beings are phenomenal when they put their heads together and collaborate. Here's a short list of some human achievements that were accomplished when pressing to have a *ruthless dedication* to a cause.

My argument is that if you're going to launch your personal brand, do it in 90 days. It's a long enough time frame for progress to take place, a long enough runway for you to make the all the possible screw-ups required to understand how to grow a personal brand—mistakes that I will remedy by giving you a framework of thinking and specific tools to take action in the next chapters of this book. Take note: mistakes are inevitable. Failure must be welcomed with open arms, because it's a standard ingredient to success, to gaining experience, and to learning what's necessary to achieve something valuable in life.

I launched my personal brand in just 90 days:

- I started posting content daily from day 1, with about 400 followers made up of friends and family.
- I had 1,000 followers by week 2.
- I had my products and services established by week 4.
- I created a steady flow of paying clients by week 6.
- I handed in my resignation at my job in week 8.
- I had locked in six retainer clients for six months, each paying me $3,500 US monthly on a retainer by week 9.
- I hired my first contractor to support the workload by week 10.
- I had more clients and $72,000 US in my bank account at week 12.

By day 90, I had completely turned my life around by building a personal brand. In just 90 days I had gone from being so broke that I couldn't afford groceries to having the luxury of hiring someone to work with me. In just 90 days I had gone from working on my busted laptop with pirated software to buying expensive equipment with all the software I wanted. In just 90 days I had gone from doing all the work myself to delegating the majority of the workload to my contractors—while I handled all the client relations. In just 90 days I had gone from being afraid, full of doubt and self-loathing to exuding confidence, excitement, and being full of aspiration for the future. In just 90 days I had gone from posting pictures of my dog Zeus and me on the beach to being seen as an expert at branding.

I'm not here to brag, and I'm not saying that it's easy, because it's not—and that's precisely why it's worth doing. If I can go from flipping phones for a living to working with clients globally inside 90 days, then so can you. I'm simply here to show that it's possible if you want it badly enough, if you put in the relentless dedication it takes to make it happen. So, rather than taking it easy and attempting to constantly keep balance in your life, I suggest you try something new, something you've never done before. And do it in 90 days.

90 days is a long enough time frame to do the following:

* See your follower count grow. It's a long enough time to experiment and test different ideas in order to find "your thing" (your niche).
* Figure out what products and services you will sell.
* Connect with a large group of people (your tribe) and listen to their needs, fears, concerns, and desires—then pair your product/service offering to match their language.
* Try different types of content to test different ways of designing, writing, or filming; it's enough time for you to learn the ropes of how social media actually works.
* Make mistakes and turn things around again.
* Find people and entities you can partner with along your journey.
* Monetize yourself in order to save it and invest it back into your strategy and plan.
* Upskill yourself on creativity, writing, filming, editing, posting, writing captions, learning hashtags.
* Study what works for other people that you can copy and implement for yourself.
* Gain confidence in seeing that what you're doing is working.
* Have posted a lot of content to then later review regarding what's working and what's not working.
* Test different sales techniques to discover the best approach to talking to your sort of client.
* Get a website up and running with ads in order to supplement what you're doing with your social media content.

- Hire consultants, train them, and have them assist you in growing your business.
- Learn which ads work and which ads don't.
- Launch that podcast of yours.
- Start creating some credibility for yourself so that people respect you.
- Prove your haters and doubters wrong.
- Prove to your spouse, parents, friends, family that what you're doing is actually working and that they should encourage you.
- Replace your income so that you can quit the job you hate.
- Develop, ship, and launch a product with an e-commerce store.
- Get a loan from a bank to go all in on your ideas; or, if the bank won't give you a loan . . .
  - . . . sell all your furniture to raise the capital to invest in your idea.
  - . . . sell your house and car, move into a rental, and use that equity to invest in your idea.
  - . . . find multiple investors to pitch your ideas to and raise the capital to start your venture.

Ninety days is also simultaneously a short enough time frame for you to crash and burn, fail completely, dust yourself off, hit reset, take two weeks off to recover (crying in the fetal position), then do it all over again for a total of four times in one year. Sounds fun, right?

The worst case in the immediate sense is that your social page doesn't grow, you spend a bunch of time producing content that nobody looks at or cares about, people don't buy your products and services, and a few negative people make fun of you, snickering in the shadows. None of which will matter when you're on your deathbed in your 90s. If your 90-day game plan doesn't succeed, it doesn't mean that you won't ever succeed—it just means you need to adapt and change your approach. It's better to discover your idea doesn't work in 90 days than waiting a few years before even giving it a go. If you can fail fast and fail forward in a compressed time frame, you learn. You've had the blessing of learning what doesn't work and you learned it quickly. The dirty thief of success is procrastination, which leads to never trying in the first place.

According to *Inc.*, "the 25 richest Americans [as of 2014] failed miserably"[13] in their business pursuits multiple times before they reached the top. Even if you were to fail 14 times, you can still have enough time to bounce back each time. The idea here is that if you're going to fail 14 businesses, fail them all in 90 days; 14 separate 90-day brand plans equate to only 1,260 days, so if you divide that by years it's just under 3.5 years, which means that within your third year in business you would have drastically increased your chances of success to find that one thing that works for you.

Conquer Procrastination

Let's say you're thinking, *"But, Dain, what if I burn out?"* I would say, "Take a hard look at yourself in the mirror and tell yourself, 'I'm not a candle'"— and repeat this to yourself every day until you believe it. You're not going to burn out quickly. Not as long as you have a fire in your belly to succeed, enough pain in your circumstances to get off your ass, and a good enough reason to get started.

Humans sometimes choose the easier route of procrastination (the thief of success, remember?). If you can get out of your own head, and get into taking constant daily action, you'll then, and only then, be able to reach your complete potential (mistakes and all) and give it everything you have got for 90 days.

A hell of a lot can happen in rapid succession when you compress time frames, become nonnegotiable on your goals, and feed your mind with the fuel it needs to grow. When I say that you should compress your time frames, what I mean is that you should do the work required to build your business as efficiently and in as little time as possible through daily massive action and consistency.

The 90-day brand plan is about attacking the market with everything you've got and stopping at nothing to make it happen on your own terms. The 90-day brand plan is a springboard into doing what you love every day. It's a starting mechanism, a spark to ignite the fuel in your tank so that you can get moving. It's about teaching you to get out of your head and into your body, working on your goals. It's about taking action over thinking. It's about saying no to distractions and going all in on discipline. The 90-day brand plan is about saying "enough" to waiting for life to go your way and taking control of the ship.

Exercise: Imagine Your Future Self

For this first exercise I want you to keep things simple. Think of a big goal you desire for your personal brand—for example, giving speeches, launching a company, reaching 10,000 followers, and so on.

Then write down what you believe has been holding you back from succeeding at that goal.

Write down your biggest goal for your personal brand:

| |
| |

Write down the 10 things holding you back from starting:

1.	
2.	
3.	
4.	
5.	
6.	
7.	
8.	
9.	
10.	

If you didn't put yourself at the top of the list as the reason why you're not succeeding, then you need to reevaluate and place yourself as the sole proprietor for the reason you don't have it. The moment you take full responsibility for not being in full pursuit of going for your desired goal, you take back control of your story and the ownership over your goal. The idea here is to hijack your excuses with one name on the list, and that's your name. Just as I did, you can have 1,000 reasons why you can't do something, but you only need one reason to do something. And that starts with you.

This is why the 90-day brand plan is so valuable. It's about wholeheartedly investing in yourself and cultivating the confidence you need to realize that you're solely responsible for not just your failures but also your success. Nobody is going to save you. Nobody is going to do it for you. Throwing money at the problem won't fix the root cause. It's purely your duty, your obligation, and your quest to do this for yourself.

My suggestion is that you scrap the whole list and keep a reminder that you're in control. Create a memento that keeps you accountable, whatever that looks like to you. For me, it used to a card that I kept in my pocket that just had my name on it. It reminded me that I was solely responsible for everything I had in life. Now, it's a tattoo on my left arm with a quote from author Ryan Holiday that reads "THE OBSTACLE IS THE WAY."

Chapter Summary

I reflect on the fact that Rivyl was an intentional by-product of my personal brand. Starting as a mere idea in my head, it has ended up by having a massive impact on my career and life. I've grown it to a team of more than 20 creative individuals, who work as a collaborative team that streamlines my ideas and processes. I also outline that the power of personal branding and how it supersedes the influence of corporate branding. People are far more interested in human beings than they are in corporate brands or entities.

I go on to explain how developing and fostering a successful personal brand helped me gain credibility, attract clients, and secure opportunities with industry giants. I also encourage anyone reading to really go out of your way to leverage social media in your personal branding journey, no matter what you're doing—whether that's starting a business, looking for a job, or anything else. And if you're going to make a true effort to start a personal brand, you should do it for 90 days.

The 90-Day Brand Plan is an intense, focused, and accelerated approach to personal branding. It ensures that you can get everything you need in a shorter time frame, from celebrating victories to learning from your losses. It's about ensuring that you grow in the most efficient way possible. It's about getting rid of distractions and putting your all into a persistent and calculated pursuit.

Free Chapter 1 Resources

I've designed a helpful guide to help you navigate this chapter's more in-depth and interactive sections. If you want to explore this in more detail, go to **dainwalker.com/resources/chpt1.** It's totally free, so make sure you don't miss out. You can also scan the QR code to get access.

Chapter 2

LEAVE YOUR COMFORT ZONE

"Failure is success in progress."

—Albert Einstein

Before going any further into how to begin building your **personal brand**, it's important that you understand that you don't have to have accomplished something remarkable to build one—you can start from nothing. I know this because I started from nothing. I hope this story of my beginning shatters any reluctance you feel and replaces it with relentless optimism.

I never viewed myself as someone exceptional. I didn't view myself as someone who had the "gift of the gab," and I certainly didn't see myself as some kind of guru. What I did have however was the willingness to summon the courage to wander in a direction I'd never gone in before. I needed to leave my comfort zone, and I learned that I needed to get comfortable with leaving it, constantly.

I was tired of "playing it safe" and feeling that I needed to find the perfect plan for where I should begin. I decided to start seeking a healthy relationship with failure as a necessity to my journey and all the valuable lessons that came with it. I was willing to take complete responsibility for my life. Finally, I was willing to go all out with everything I had for 90 days as an experiment, with an open mind to see what was possible.

This is my story of how I went from **basement** to **boardroom**.

 ## Finding My Basement

I checked the fuel gauge every two minutes, adjusting my speed to make sure I didn't burn more fuel than was needed. Burning extra fuel would mean digging into our weekly grocery money to pay for it. My fiancée, Elli, and I were already struggling to make ends meet with our combined debt and two average-paying wages. We were on a two-hour road trip, driving in the morning from the Sunshine Coast to Brisbane, Australia, heading to a keynote event to see Gary Vaynerchuck (known as Gary Vee).

For those who don't know, Gary Vee is an entrepreneur who owns his own media agency called VaynerMedia. He rose to success after starting his own YouTube channel called WineLibraryTV, where he produced an episode every day for almost five years straight. He began to give keynotes in 2008, wrote his own successful book in 2009, and went on to become a very successful thought leader in the entrepreneurial space. His following has grown to such an extent that he now dominates Instagram, YouTube, LinkedIn, and TikTok. As with my lifelong goal of running a successful agency, Gary's life ambition is to buy the New York Jets.

Anyway, my friend Rob had convinced me to go to Gary's event. But, despite being a huge fan of Gary Vee, I was initially annoyed that I'd agreed. Why was I wasting our precious hard-earned money on fuel to get there?

Frustrated with myself, my thoughts wandered to how I should get a second job—as a night janitor, maybe?—so we could get ahead a bit. I felt like I was failing Elli. I hated that we spent our evenings together deciding toward which debt we should put every cent we'd earned. With every new payday, every dollar was pre-allocated. And yet here we were, wasting fuel.

Staring at the highway ahead, I wondered why we were going. I dreamed of owning a business, but how could I start a company if I couldn't even put food on the table? What kind of business could I possibly start? Where should I start? And shouldn't I conquer my debt before branching into the world of business?

At the time I sold mobile phones. Before that, I managed a gym location for a franchise. The founder had promised me equity in the franchise if I could commit to several years at one of his locations. I'd agreed but then pulled out; it just didn't feel like the right industry for me. (Not to mention, I'd be committing to two years in a small country town for just 10% equity in a gym that was in the red every month.) To invest so much time for such little reward at too high a risk—it just didn't add up. There had to be a better way.

If I hadn't agreed to go to this event—that I'll admit, Rob had *demanded* I attend—Elli and I would have ventured to second-hand stores to buy wooden tables for about $25. Back at home in our garage, I'd sand them by hand, give them a fresh lick of paint, and then sell them online for $200 to $300 a pop—which was just enough every week to put an extra dent in our debt. "But you have to go," Rob insisted. "It's Gary, man!" so I obliged and reluctantly spent the $390 for tickets to attend "Success Resources 2019," which felt like all the money we had.

Arriving at the event, packed with over 5,000 guests, I swiveled my head in amazement. I was here now, and eager to learn—pen and paper in hand—so I started jotting down notes from each speaker. But before long, I stopped taking notes. Speaker after speaker, all entrepreneurs, berated the audience with their sales pitches, bootcamps, and programs. After each talk, the stage filled with people making testimonials about how the last speaker had "changed their life," and if it weren't for them, they would never have succeeded. And—as long as I had $15,000 or so to invest, I could be "just like them!" But $15,000 was an impossible feat for us at that time. Disengaging from the spectacle, I shifted my attention to the energy of the room. After five hours of this onslaught, the audience sat there with their arms crossed, their faces frowned, totally unmoved.

But one speaker did grab my attention, someone whose books I'd enjoyed, promoting a bootcamp at a discount that lasted exclusively for the next five minutes: Grant Cardone. Elli whispered, "You should do it. You love him, and you've always said if he ever comes to Australia you'd go." With Elli's encouragement, and "only four more minutes!" I decided: "Fuck it, maybe this is what I need to do!"

I ran over to the kiosk where an attendee was handing out paperwork. When I asked about payment plans she replied, "Sure! Just four installments of $3,500 on a biweekly repayment." My jaw hit the floor, my excitement crushed. I really wanted to go but I just couldn't afford it.

Elli immediately "needed to go to the bathroom"—which I found out later meant that she cried for 45 minutes in that bathroom, feeling guilty about our combined debt and ashamed that she couldn't help me. "The look on your face broke my heart," she said. "We're in this together," I replied. "We'll figure something out."

I returned to my seat, humiliated, frustrated, beetroot red, even considering leaving early. My heart sank as my head raced; I'd wasted $390 on tickets, $55 on fuel, $10 on coffee, and a whole day that I could have spent making a table to flip for $300. I was down $755. Which meant another week of budgeting food and clock-watching my fuel gauge.

I walked out to the foyer to blow another $5 on coffee to distract myself. I thought, *"Why am I so upset? It's just a bootcamp, dude; get over it. So what if you can't afford it; just go home and keep doing what you're doing."* But something interesting happened at that moment. I decided, rather than deflect my pain and distract myself . . . maybe I should sit with it. Maybe I should reflect on this and listen to my emotions, maybe there was a lesson to be learned in all of this.

I decided to lean into it. I sat with my emotions and asked myself, *"Yeah . . . why am I upset?"* I waited, feeling humiliation in my chest, feeling my blood pumping in frustration. I sat in my pain and confronted it—this feeling that had been hidden under the surface for so long that I'd always ignored but now was very loud and unavoidable. I replied to myself, *"I don't want to feel like this ever again. I don't want to be humiliated and not to be able to afford something I desperately want ever again. I never want to be broke again. It's time to approach things differently. It's time to get off your ass and do something about it.* Then I heard a voice saying, "Dain . . . Dain . . ." My order was ready.

As the barista handed me my latte, I heard a huge commotion. I turned to watch people flooding back into the room like a herd of buffalo, hundreds cramming through the door into the event. Gary Vee was up next. Rather than returning to our seats I stood at the back of the room with my coffee. Gary ran out on stage and opened: "What's up, Brisbane?!" followed by a roaring standing ovation. He leaned over the edge of the stage and said, smiling, "Guess what?! I'm not here to sell you shit!" Boom! He immediately had my attention.

The room had gone from snoozeville to electrified. All seats were filled, the aisles lined with people from the stage to the back of the room. After an entire day of speakers, each with a suit, a keynote, a laser pointer, and testimonials, here was Gary, in a snapback, sneakers, and a pair of jeans. All Gary did was share his story for 10 minutes—no keynote slides or anything—then proceeded with Q&A for more than two hours. The audience was in pure anticipation the entire time, standing on their seats, filming on their phones, furiously writing notes, fully and wholeheartedly engaged.

What the hell just happened? Nobody else was able to win the crowd in its entirety, but Gary did it in a heartbeat, without a keynote, and with what seemed like zero preparation. I was awestruck. I was baffled. Why the hell didn't anyone else own the stage like Gary did?

Later I looked at all their social media pages and realized something: all the other speakers produced content in order to sell something. But Gary didn't. He was only interested in helping his audience start their journey, whatever it was. He essentially just wanted to push people into just starting.

But that's what I learned later. At the time, during that Q&A session, one thing pierced my skull like a bolt of lightning, where it's sizzled ever since:

"You don't need to attend one of these stupid bootcamps to start a business. You just need to decide, you just need to commit, you just need to be patient, and you just need to *fucking start*."

—*Gary Vee*

It was like Gary had just lit a match under the frustrated emotional pain I'd been sitting with: "*I never want to be broke again. It's time to approach things differently. It's time to get off your ass and do something about it—'Just fucking start!'*"

DRIVING BACK, MY FOOT FLAT ON THE GAS PEDAL IN A RUSH TO GET HOME, I NO LONGER GAVE A FUCK ABOUT FUEL. I confessed everything to Elli: "That's it, I'm done feeling sorry for myself. I'm starting a business the SECOND we get home!" "Great," Elli replied. "What business?" I sat with her question for a few seconds and it spilled out. "I'm starting an agency, and we will become the biggest creative agency in Australia" (a little audacious, right?).

Starting from My Basement

As you can see from my story, I had nothing to start with. No credibility, no track record, no awards or accolades, no money, no clients, no testimonials. So who the hell was I to start an agency—of any kind?

This is what I mean when I say I started my brand in the basement:

- I'd never worked for an agency, ever.
- I had zero experience as a freelancer.
- I had no idea how to start a business.
- I had no money to invest into my idea.
- I had a slow laptop that barely worked.

- All my income went toward debt. All of it.
- I worked long hours and had limited free time.
- None of my friends could offer professional advice.
- I had no idea where to start in general.
- I couldn't afford to pay someone to coach me.
- I didn't know a thing about the risks or problems in this industry.
- I had no idea what my products would be.
- I had no plan on how I was going to monetize it.
- I had never sold creative service-based products before.
- I had never consulted for business owners before.
- I had no idea where I would even get clients.
- I had no legal means to get the software I needed.

You get the picture, right? I'm telling you, if I'd applied for a job at any agency with this as my experience level, my résumé would not only have been rejected—it would have been laughed at. I had nothing.

You can wander outside the safety parameters of your comfort zone if there's something you want badly enough. Sometimes in life, however, we need a push to make it happen. Whatever your push moment is, allow it to speak to you; don't ignore your inner voice when it arrives. Don't succumb to imposter syndrome before you even start.

I want to say a bit about what imposter syndrome is and how we can deal with it.

According to the *Cambridge Dictionary*, imposter syndrome is *"the persistent inability to believe that one's success is deserved or has been legitimately achieved as a result of one's own effort or skills."*[1]

I get this question about imposter syndrome all the time. My answer: just start; act like a student and post content (more on this in Chapter 3: Slay the Time Vampires). You must approach your personal branding journey like you're studying and not mastering. Because you are. Until you're a master, you're a student. And to remain a master, guess what? You still have to be a student.

Ultimately, when starting a personal brand, no matter your situation, some part of you will feel like an imposter. I've yet to meet a student or client who didn't experience some form of feeling like an imposter when starting. Some people always feel it. And it's not a condition reserved for those of us with zero credibility; it's universal. I've seen it at all levels, from wealthy, successful people with business acumen to people who are just starting out.

But what I constantly see is that those who persist despite feeling like imposters soon realize that the feeling can fade away. The monster of judgment in your head gets defanged and eventually leaves you alone (for the most part). And when it does rear its ugly ass head, remind yourself why you started in the first place. That's all you need to know to start.

To build your personal brand is to actualize your future self into the present. By thinking about whom you wish to become in the future and embodying that person now, you're priming yourself to start acting accordance to your goals. Here are a few questions to get you started:

- How would you speak to and address people?
- How would you look?
- How would you want others to feel about you?
- How would you behave?

Similar to an actor learning their role in a movie, you need to get into the role of acting as your future self on social media and act that role right now. Give yourself permission: you've won the casting call and have earned the role. Your paycheck will soon be in the mail. And don't do it for your friends and family—act the role for your future adoring fans. It makes it less scary—I promise.

THE DAY AFTER THE GARY VEE EVENT, I STARTED SCOUTING THE INTERNET to see what other agency owners were doing with their personal brands. I needed to understand high-level personal branding to truly know how to model myself, to truly follow the success of others to eventually carve out my own path to success. This is the entire crux of this book: to give you the push that I needed, and the information to just start. I also began to post content a week after the event and continued to post for 90 days in a row. (More on this in Chapter 3: Slay the Time Vampires.)

Just Start

So, despite your fears, despite your shortcomings, you need to simply make a decision, and that's it—a declaration of whom you wish to become. Once you realize that life is not about "finding motivation" and that it's actually about *creating yourself*, then you can start to build whatever you want. That's the beauty of personal branding: you get to decide whom you become, what you want to be known for, and what you want to build. You get to start with a blank canvas and paint whatever you want on it. So no matter your personal situation, lack of experience, or shortcomings, you just need to **decide** to start.

Building your brand starts with the ability to turn off the part of your brain that says, "You can't do that." Because the reality is that you can.

Think of it like being a student of an art form. As a student, your role is simply attending. And attending class for a personal brand begins with producing content to share with others. If you think like a student, you won't feel the pressure to perform like a master. When you do meet masters, you'll be surprised that the majority of them still act and behave like students, always testing new concepts, always learning, always adapting to what's happening with new platforms, and adjusting on the fly. See, if you act like a student, it takes away all the pressure.

In the beginning I never proclaimed to be an expert at anything. I merely just started posting content on a topic that interested me. Once you've posted something on the internet, it's beyond your control. It's not your job to interpret what your content means. It's just your job to pay attention to how people react and adjust your approach in real time as you go while working on yourself like a student works on improving their grades.

The weirdest part of my experience in doing this was realizing that the people who were the most interested in my content weren't my friends. The people who commented, engaged, liked, shared, and spread the word the most weren't my colleagues or my family—they were complete strangers halfway across the globe. They judged me based on my content and whether it was valuable to them or not. Your personal brand, to them, is a valuable commodity. They don't have a preconceived perception of you. You get to create one from scratch.

This is all to say that once you're mentally prepared to embark on your personal branding journey, you can begin arming yourself with your survival tool kit. To understand these tools, I will continue to unpack the personal branding journey through a series of thematic frameworks and metaphors. Here's your next exercise.

Exercise: Cast Your Future Self

The goal is to keep the character you're now developing yourself to be top of mind as you slowly craft and work on yourself to build a consistent personality style for your audience to connect with.

Your answers don't need to be long. I encourage you to simply write them down and return to them frequently. Note too that it's common for people to change their answers as they start producing content and explore different methods of creating content.

So, with the freedom of knowing you might change your answers later, it's important that you challenge yourself now and take the time to be as specific as possible.

I like to keep this exercise simple because it is subject to so much change. It's a tool I strongly encourage you to frequently return to, to adapt to your personal brand. All you want to do here is write down single-word adjectives, descriptive words that highlight how you wish to model your future self. You'll find examples listed next to help you get started. Choose whatever words are most fitting for the person you wish to become, not where you are right now.

Write down six things that describe the personal brand you wish to become.

1. How will you speak?

For example: seriously, commandingly, friendly, humorously, candidly, etc.

2. What will you dress like?

For example: casual, professional, suburban, glammed-up, etc.

3. How will you make people feel?

For example: confident, unashamed, excitied, empowered, mystified, etc.

4. How will you behave?

For example: expressive, calm, direct, energetic, etc.

5. What do you believe in?

For example: helping others, entertaining others, informing others, educating others, etc.

6. What impact will you make?

For example: help one billion people learn how to monetize their personal brands with accesible educational resources

Chapter Summary

I begin by emphasizing that building a personal brand has no prerequisites. It can start from nothing and become something incredible. In my own personal experience, I talk about how my willingness to leave my comfort zone was an incredible asset, as was my newfound ability to embrace failures as part of the process.

I speak candidly about my initial financial struggles and how attending an event that Gary Vee spoke at shifted my entire perspective. His transparency and directness sparked a realization. It made me acutely aware of the fact that nothing was stopping me from "just fucking starting." It was the catalyst and origin story of my branding agency Rivyl.

I continue by highlighting my rise from my "basement" to the eventual "boardroom" of Rivyl. In doing this, I explore the crippling power of imposter syndrome and how I learned to overcome it by acting like a student, constantly learning and consistently producing content without making excuses. It's all about starting despite your fears and potential initial shortcomings, not succumbing to self-doubt. I realized the power of sitting with your emotions and listening to yourself. Personal branding is ultimately a journey of continuous self-creation.

I end by presenting the idea that to truly visualize and actualize success, you need to cast your future self and think about how you want to sound, look, and feel to others, not how you currently hold yourself. True success comes from making sure you have a clear vision to follow, and that clear vision needs to be a future version of you that's enjoying the success that you wish to have.

Free Chapter 2 Resources

I've designed a helpful guide to help you navigate this chapter's more in-depth and interactive secB tions. If you want to explore this in more detail, go to **dainwalker.com/resources/chpt2.** It's totally free, so make sure you don't miss out. You can also scan the QR code to get access.

SCAN ME

Chapter 3

SLAY THE TIME VAMPIRES

Branding is complicated. It can feel overwhelming and challenging to grasp as a concept. So I've created a "campfire to empire" framework to make the information as retainable and understandable as possible. You won't need any experience whatsoever in marketing, content creation, branding, advertising, or sales in order to implement what I'm teaching here. You also won't need to study any other books on branding—let alone attain a degree—in order to master this. Unlike branding as a whole, this framework is simple, it's down to earth, and it's practical.

The Campfire-to-Empire Framework

Think about it like this: in deciding to develop your personal brand, you've essentially opted to leave the safety of comfortability and normality—to journey out into the wilderness on your own and survey the world of personal branding. Think of it like this: every personal brand has its own patch of land—each with its own niche, specialty, offering, product service, and unique way of seeing the world. Some are better than others, and some are bigger than others. Personal brands can range from sports to business, psychology, music, movies, education, academia—the list is endless.

Each of these personal brands had to start their own campfire out in the wilderness. Initially alone with zero followers, nobody listening to them, they sat by their little campfire alone, throwing on a log occasionally to keep the fire burning. The majority who do this quit—overcome by the sheer difficulty of designing and executing a personal brand consistently.

However, a dedicated few push through the discomfort and discouragement, learning how to slowly but surely surround their fire with adoring fans who love their work, love their story, and love them.

That campfire of each personal brand represents their content, whatever it is they're producing. It could be a blog, a vlog, a social media page, or a website with a newsletter. If they're a comedian, the stage is their campfire. Your content, whatever it is, is a campfire. Each piece of content is a log in the fire to keep your personal brand alive and burning. Over time your campfire will start drawing a crowd out of the wilderness.

Each person who comes to sit and find warmth from your fire is an admirer of your content; those who become dedicated admirers—dedicated members of your target audience—essentially become tribe members, and later, adoring fans. (Others might enjoy hating you from the shadows just outside your campfire, but we won't worry about them; they still serve the algorithm and drive traffic to your page. Praise be the algorithm.) There are many different types of tribe members. Some will just want to watch, and some will want to comment and engage. Some tribe members want to participate and help you on your journey: advertising you, promoting you, endorsing you, and following you into battle wherever you go. Your goal is to build an audience, to find fans, to grow, to nourish, and to cultivate a tribe of devoted followers (some will even eventually pay you).

Establish Consistency

As you continue to make content—at least one piece of content per day for 90 days—each piece is a log placed on your campfire. And as your tribe begins to grow, so will your campfire, meaning, your tribe will demand more content from you. More logs on the fire. Previously just a few sticks in the dirt, your campfire will start to evolve. Stones will be added to it and it will burn brighter, taller, and gain momentum in its growth.

But note: your goal as a personal brand is not to demand anything from your tribe, but to serve them. Keep them warm by giving them value, telling them stories, listening to their problems, serving their needs, and eventually inspiring them to make their lives better through your log offerings to the algorithm (praise be the algorithm).

Eventually, your campfire will transform into a village—which is when you'll be able to take your small entourage of tribe members and turn your campfire into a village that's commoditized and monetized. In the next chapters, you'll learn how to have your tribe WANT to give you money in exchange for the value they get from your entertainment, your education, and your support.

Just like different types of wood will burn in your fire, you're free to decide which combination of content will keep your community warm. And if you do it right, your particular combination will be unlike anyone else's.

This uniquely crafted idea branches into other concepts, such as collaborations between your campfire and other personal brand campfires, how to connect your tribe to other tribes, and how to have other tribes find you.

In time, you'll learn how to scout your environment, how to explore it for resources, and how to capitalize on those resources. More on this later. For now, we're just getting started.

Scout the Landscape

Picture this: plotting how to grow your brand is like rolling out a giant map and staring at its landscape. Where and how should you set up your campfire in the short term? Where and how do you want to build your empire in the long term? These are big decisions. How could you possibly know where to choose if you've never even scouted the area before? I suggest you scout the terrain a little to get acquainted with what others are doing in your space. Where is the audience currently congregating in your niche? Who has the attention? And where is money being made? By doing this sort of reconnaissance prior to igniting your very own campfire, you can gain insights from those who are already succeeding with what you want to do.

But before we go out scouting—which we'll do in Chapter 4: Scout Industries, Model People—we need to prepare your tool kit. We need to make sure you have your affairs in order before we venture out into the wilderness and start building your brand. To help you prepare, I've laid out some of the key tools for your survival kit. These are things that greatly affected how I was able to get so much momentum in my first 90 days—tools I still use today to keep me focused. Following that, I've also highlighted the key elements of the mindset necessary for not just surviving the 90-day challenge but finding ways to enjoy it and thrive in it. A challenge should be fun, and building a business can be fun. It all comes down to the mindset you adopt each day you put yourself out there creating content, throwing logs on the fire, and growing your personal brand.

Your 90-Day Tool Kit

If you were actually planning to spend 90 days out in the wilderness—far away from cellular towers and out of wireless range—you would expect to take a break from your regular habits of consuming all that tech offers us. You'll want to do the same for this 90-day sprint, even if you never leave your bedroom.

I refer to the kinds of things that can distract us from our goals as *time vampires*: they suck up the time we need to get to where we want to be. And they're everywhere, seemingly invisible and drastically effective at postponing our big goals. And though they're time-consuming, they're not all inherently *bad*. They can come in the form of people to spend time with, hobbies we love to spend time on. But they also can come in the form of meaningless distractions that steal hours out of our days without really thinking about it, from time spent idly surfing the web to chores we could outsource—or at least put off until next quarter. Time vampires will slow your progress and distance you from opportunities, so it's important that you start becoming extremely conscious of where each hour of your day is being invested. Make what was invisible to you yesterday extremely visible today and tomorrow.

I recommend that you plan—for 90 days—to limit, cut back, or even completely cut out any distractions that block your path to success. This can sound dramatic, but that's the point. Maybe it's time you get a little dramatic with your goals. I realized when I started my journey that taking it easy wasn't doing anything for me. I needed to drastically change my behavior, actions, and mindset about how I was investing my time—because time is an investment. I needed to be honest with myself and carefully track how much time each week I dedicated to distractions.

Slay Your Vampires

When I first did this, I'll be honest . . . it was painful to actually calculate the time I invested in things that weren't serving me, such as video games, apps, entertainment, social outings, and so on. Although these things were enjoyable and gave me joy in life, my financial situation brought me pain, and ultimately, too much indulgence stood in the way of me getting to where I wanted to be.

I like to think of it like this: every day we have 24 one-hour tokens to invest. How we choose to invest each token maps out our future lives. I like to call these tokens *fuel tokens* because they create and fuel your campfire's success. You're either wasting your fuel or using it. If you want to accomplish great things, you must dedicate as many fuel tokens as possible toward your cause—every day. That means changing "I'm too busy" to "I'll find time" or "I can't do this" to "I'll make it work." Out of everything I've done to create my personal brand, slaying my time vampires and becoming hypervigilant about where I invest my fuel tokens has made me more money and grown my company more than I thought was possible.

Here's a list of time vampires for you to consider slaying while you focus on your 90-day brand plan:

Unplug and pack away your video game/entertainment systems. I personally love gaming. It's a great way to rest my brain and blow off some steam, but I frequently spent three-plus hours gaming—every day. That was precious time I could have instead dedicated to producing content and generating leads. And, trust me, it's not enough to just unplug your equipment. You have to box it up, out of reach, in order to remove the temptation and break the habit.

Cancel entertainment subscriptions. One of my biggest distractions was to binge-watch shows on television with Elli—for hours on end. So it was really tough to cut this cord, for the first three days especially. But removing the entertainment option is as empowering as it is scary. After about a week, I found I was seeking my dopamine thrills from my work instead, and Elli and I were actually happier. So although this one might feel tough initially, it's worth it.

Uninstall apps on your phone. Apps are sneaky time vampires. You may spend just 8 minutes here, 12 minutes there . . . but those small numbers can add up to hours. So browse your phone for apps that you frequent. With a quick settings check, your smartphone will tell you how much time you dedicate to each of your apps—confronting you with sheer numbers. If the app doesn't serve your goal, remove it. And for the social apps that do serve your goal, consider changing the settings with daily limits, so they boot you off before you get too sucked in.

Limit social outings and events. One of the biggest time vampires is social outings and events. Sure, it's important to have connection and comradery with loved ones, but I had to take a hard stance with how broke I was. I decided that, unless something immediately contributed to my 90-day brand plan and added fuel to my campfire, it got a rain check. It's not that Elli and I weren't social at all—we just spent much less time being social. Now, this is much more feasible if you don't have children, because children need quality time with their parents. (I talk about this more in the next section.)

If you're willing to put in the 90 days to the best of your ability—if you're looking to move the needle in life from frustration to success—then it's time to slay your time vampires. They'll still be there if you so choose to return to them.

Boost Your Amplifiers

Replace entertainment with education. Instead of gaming or doomscrolling on your phone, consider replacing entertainment with educational content—some of which, despite being educational, can also be entertaining. Instead of bingeing a series on Netflix, binge a master class and take notes. Instead of listening to music during a long drive or workout routine, listen to audio tapes that touch on the specific skills you wish to improve.

Though entertainment content is enjoyable and engaging, making this shift to educational content challenged me to alter my belief systems and behaviors. I was inspired to confront my problems and tackle them head-on, and I found value in books and courses that challenged me to think, act, and behave with a bigger frame of mind.

Notify loved ones. Now, before you plough ahead with your 90-day brand plan, remember that your closest loved ones are essentially coming along for the journey, because what you're doing will affect them in some way. They may not be happy about your altered behavior and activities, especially if it impedes their lifestyle. It's natural for loved ones to question the sudden shift in lifestyle, so it's wise to respect that and, especially, to not force them to participate in your new activities. I recommend that you share with your loved ones the why behind what you're doing: why it's important to you, what inspired you to do it, and how much it means to you to pursue it. Better yet, explain the potential rewards for them at the end of the 90 days. For example, a student of mine hired a chef for their wife after the 90 days; another took their kids to Disneyland. Offering a post-90-day reward can motivate your family to support you during your challenge, especially in moments of doubt when you need it most.

Find an accountability partner. Accountability is a powerful survival tool for your 90-day brand plan, especially for those who initially struggle with self-accountability. So enlist someone to be your accountability partner—someone willing to receive calls or texts from you at the beginning and end of all 90 days of your challenge.

With the morning message you'll inform them of your goals for the day; with the evening message you'll inform them of your progress. And in the event they haven't heard from you by some set time, they'll contact you to give you a pep talk and remind you of why you took this challenge. So you want to find someone who's not a pushover, someone who won't accept your excuses and let you slack off. Choose someone who'll push you to strive outside your comfort zone—and then celebrate with you when you do it.

Start journaling. The idea of keeping a journal is to write down ideas and inspiration as soon as they come to you. Journaling is an exercise you'll want to get comfortable with; you may think you can retain everything in your head, but I know from experience there is only so much you can recall—and I've definitely lost some great ideas from not writing them down. A great tip I discovered is to write down the time, day, and where you were when you made your notes; this will help you remember everything better.

I can't tell you the number of times I sat down, ready to create content, and my mind went blank—only to flick open my journal and find an ocean of ideas. I would often use my journal to write down failures and successes and what I learned from them. I recorded and refined my goals and content. As a result I managed to ideate more things that I then combined to create more content.

Now, I prefer a physical notebook. I recommend you buy yourself a nice journal, something captivating that you'll want to pick up and write in, and then carry it with you at all times. (Just don't lose it.) Of course, some prefer to record their ideas digitally; that works, too. No matter the choice, find what works for you and stay consistent.

Start a calendar. If I had to identify the wooden stake that consistently slayed and continues to slay my time vampires, it was the fact that I methodically prepared and organized my calendar—and stuck to it. The goal is to log into your calendar how much time you spend on everything you do, every day. For example:

- Bathing/grooming/self-care
- Preparing and eating food
- Commuting/traveling
- On phone calls/in meetings
- Creating content
- Growing your social page
- Self-education
- Consuming content/entertainment
- Socializing/outings
- Connecting with loved ones
- Resting and sleeping

When maintained honestly and wholeheartedly, your calendar—whether it's an app on your phone or a spiral notebook—will keep you extremely accountable to yourself. Nothing beats having a calendar convey the sheer facts of everything you completed of what you committed to. But the idea is not to punish yourself; it's to identify and remove whatever time vampires are hindering your success. It truly puts your life into perspective. Whenever anyone tells me, "I don't have time," I ask them to show me their calendar. If they have one, it's usually empty. Strive to remove from your vocabulary using time as an excuse. Become a master time manager.

Calculate your fuel tokens. Once you've set up your calendar, it's important to start tracking where you spend each day's 24 one-hour fuel tokens. I find it helpful to organize these into the following five categories:

- **Family time:** This is the time you book with your loved ones. It's important that your family feels included and sees themselves as the first thing you enter into your calendar at the beginning of every week.
- **Creation time:** Being a content creator requires dedicated and allotted time with minimal distractions. I suggest breaking content creation into smaller chunks of each day rather than one giant chunk every week. I used to allot two to three hours daily for content creation and social media engagement with my followers (tribe). You'll want to sharpen your wooden stake daily and learn and improve from the previous day.
- **Money time:** Essentially, you want to calculate and log the activities that will create actual income for you, such as sales calls, presenting proposals, meeting with prospects, and so on. More on this later.
- **Operation time:** This is the time allotted to serve clients, fulfill deliverables, pay bills, and run the administration. This also includes necessary chores and errands. Anything and everything that's not covered by the money time category.
- **Personal time:** Book time for yourself. Put things in the calendar that keep you healthy, inspire you, revitalize you, and allow you to recover. Even if they are time vampires, vampires can be cool sometimes. If they fulfill you and make you happy, book it in—just be accountable for how much time you spend here. Don't overdo it.

Exercise: Check Your Tool Kit

Use this exercise to take stock of what's in your tool kit; if you prefer use a journal be my guest. Either way here's what I recommend you do:

- Identify five time vampires you're going to slay (e.g., gaming systems, entertainment subscriptions, apps on your phone or tablet, social outings, and events)—and how you're going to slay them.

- Identify which five amplifiers you're going to boost (e.g., replacing entertainment with education, notifying loved ones, finding an accountability partner, starting a calendar, and calculating fuel tokens)—and how you're going to boost them.

Here's an example answer:

- Time vampire = video gaming.
- Replacement amplifier = going to the gym.

List Five Time Vampires
1.
2.
3.
4.
5.

Notes:

List Five Replacement Amplifiers
1.
2.
3.
4.
5.

Notes:

The 90-Day Mindset

So, we've covered a lot of the processes you'll want to maintain during your 90-day challenge. Those actionable tools are essential, but they're nowhere near as effective without a solid mentality to back them up. Producing content and building a personal brand for 90 days in a row is a mind game. Whenever I encountered tough days and challenging obstacles, I frequently reminding myself of the following emotional tools to help keep me going:

Consistency: Growing your brand is not earned in a blaze of glory; it's earned in sparks and glowing embers. Each action, each post, each engagement is a tiny spark. If we lack consistency, our fire will never combust; we must constantly apply heat for our tribe to grow. Be consistent and keep adding fuel to the fire.

Patience: Continuing on that note, branding is not immediate. It takes time to build a relationship with your audience (tribe). Growing a brand calls for progressively building your image, your identity, your messaging, and your voice into your tribe's heads. This will take time to set in, which you need to be patient for. You must remember, people are extremely busy; they'll maybe give you a fraction of their day, trading you for a tiny slice of just one of their own fuel tokens. With patience and perseverance, stacking more of these moments every day, you can slowly and progressively build a personal brand that sticks in your tribe's head.

Certainty: Certainty is about wholeheartedly believing in a positive outcome. It can be difficult in the beginning—and you might honestly feel a little delusional declaring out loud what you intend to do with your brand—but being certain you'll succeed is crucial to your success. If you expect others to believe in your brand, you must first believe in your brand. This conviction and self-belief will present itself through your actions, your voice, and how you show up daily. Back yourself 100%, always see the glass as half full and follow through on your goals without hesitation.

Compassion: Have compassion for yourself. You will make mistakes—don't beat yourself up for them. Instead, give yourself a pep talk and give it another go. Don't give in. Don't judge, belittle, or taunt yourself. Don't ridicule your choices, scrutinizing what didn't work. Give yourself time and space to improve. Give yourself a safe environment to explore and experiment in. Learn from your mistakes and keep those lessons in mind as you focus on what comes next.

Adaptability: Adaptability is understanding that the wilderness of social media dishes out all types of weather. One day something works, the next day it's broken—so you adapt. Things won't always go your way. Whatever happens, use it. Don't attach to something that's not working. Be willing to change your method, approach, and style on a dime. Test new things constantly to see what leverage you can gain. Don't attach to the problems—attach yourself to what you're going to do about the problems. It bears repeating: things won't always go your way. Whatever happens, use it. Look at problems as more fuel for your campfire.

Durability: People will judge, ridicule, mock, and doubt you, even those closest to you. Humans are herd animals; when you start acting differently from the herd, they will unconsciously perceive you and your actions as a potential threat to the rest of the herd. You must ignore the temptation of giving in and resuming your "place" in the herd. Instead, encourage yourself to persist despite any conflict you encounter. Don't even bother trying to understand why you're being opposed. Instead, attach to your greater purpose, goal, and vision, and continue on.

Resourcefulness: You may not have credibility. You may not have money or even much free time on your hands. That's okay, as long as you learn how to be resourceful with what you do have. Maximize your opportunities with the time you do have, the money you may have, and the credibility you will have.

Fear: Fear is nonnegotiable. It's the compass that points at the thing that you must do. To try to ignore fear is to try to ignore your instincts—it doesn't work. So don't allow fear to fence you in; instead, use it. So many parts of building a personal brand are going to feel new to you. Things that are new can be wrapped and presented as fear. Embrace these moments, and run toward the things that terrify you. Fear is your compass pointing to the things that lay outside your comfort zone that you inherently know you must do. The reason you are fearful is that these issues typically are what you care about the most. And the things we care most about give us the most fear. That's why you should use fear as your compass; it represents what you must do in order to grow into the personal brand you wish to become.

Decisiveness: In the wild and in business, taking too long to make decisions can mean the end; getting stuck in a tailspin of paralysis analysis can blind you to opportunities and rob you of success. Complacency is the thief of joy. If you fail, so what? You gain experience points and you learn. No matter what's happening, make a decision and make it fast—immediately, if possible. If your choice didn't work out, take in the lesson; that unfavorable decision will reinforce you next time. To succeed quickly in business, being decisive is crucial.

Speed: Failing fast opens up the opportunity for fast success. You gain altitude and momentum from making many mistakes in rapid succession. In time you can evolve and adjust your approach. Pick speed over accuracy.

Tenacity: I've yet to meet a successful content creator and personal brand manager who isn't tenacious. Business is tough, content is demanding, and managing clients and employees is challenging. You must summon that fire in your belly and be ready to combat problems with conviction, power, and passion.

Ownership: Ownership is about accepting everything about yourself up until this point in your life: the good and the bad. Once you do so, you regain your power. No content creator can make this journey for you; no external individual can drive your brand. You're the captain at the helm, so you must make available the time and resources needed to grow your brand. By not blaming anyone else, by taking full responsibility for yourself and all your actions—failings and successes—you'll gain the power and resilience to resourcefully push through anything.

Momentum: Momentum is truly difficult to build and surmount—and then, once you attain it, it's incredibly easy to lose again. Momentum doesn't come from spurts of activity; it comes from constant distribution of content, constantly showing up, and continually engaging in the activities that will grow your tribe. You must find a daily rhythm that works for you. It's important that you stay engaged, pushing the momentum to move faster and bigger, never allowing the campfire to fizzle out. I've been pushing my momentum for four years and never relented. Just keep fucking going.

At the end of the day, you need to fortify yourself and your personal brand to ensure you get the most out of every day and every opportunity. It's about maximizing your time, learning how to prioritize what will serve you and abandon what will not. It's about weaponizing the 90-day mentality for the best possible outcome for your personal brand. To do that effectively, you'll need to learn how to scout your terrain and model your niche to feed not only your own passion but also grow your campfire by feeding the interests of your tribe.

Exercise: Establish Your Mindset

In order for you to embody the survival tool kit, it's important that you personalize it. By simply doing the following exercise and addressing each piece of the survival tool kit, you'll create a framework for yourself that will keep you accountable to your progress throughout the duration of your 90 days. To get the most out of this exercise, rip this page out of the book and keep it as a reminder to yourself, such as on the mirror where you brush your teeth or the back of your front door for when you leave the house. (Remember that it's good to be a little dramatic sometimes.)

The goal here is to take agency for yourself on the things that will be most essential to your mindset in the 90-day brand plan. Write down things that are personal to you. Write down things that are meaningful motivators.

90-Day Accountability Plan

I will be more patient by...

I will be more certain by...

I will have more compassion for myself by...

I will be more adaptable by...

I will be increase my durability by...

I will be more resourceful by...

I will overcome my fears by...

I will be more decisive by...

I will focus on speed by...

I will be more tenacious by...

I will take more ownership by...

I will build more momentum by...

Chapter Summary

I discuss the duality of personal branding, a complex yet altogether simple pursuit. It is complex because it is multifaceted, but simple because it can be easily understood once you have a clear understanding of your trajectory and goals. It also doesn't require any previous educational or academic knowledge or experience.

I introduce the campfire framework, a way to look at personal branding as an experience of collective growth. I expand on this by likening the production of content to throwing logs on a fire . . . a campfire. By keeping the campfire warm, you can attract your target audience. Your tribe. This is only possible through consistency and by sticking to a sprint of 90 days. *The 90-Day Brand Plan* is about paving the way for monetization strategies and methods. This is done by creating a survival tool kit that is established once you scout your industry's landscape and begin planning your future success.

I continue by introducing another two important frameworks:

- **Time vampires:** These are any aspects of your life that take away from your goals. It could be unnecessary gaming or time spent bingeing an unhelpful show.
- **Fuel tokens:** This is a framework by which you can outline your day. We all have 24 single one-hour tokens that we can use throughout the day. We need to use them wisely.

I outline the success as following a clear accelerated mindset, only possible by adhering to several metrics and goals for success:

- **Consistency:** This ensures the incremental nature of brand growth.
- **Patience:** Personal brand building takes time and patience, especially when building relationships with your tribe.
- **Certainty:** You need to believe in positive outcomes and convey that belief through all your actions.
- **Compassion:** You need self-compassion, recognizing that mistakes are part of every successful journey.
- **Adaptability:** You need to adapt to the ever-changing landscape of social media and the algorithm (praise be the algorithm).

- **Durability:** You need unwavering resilience in the face of potential judgment, doubt, and ridicule from others.
- **Resourcefulness:** You need to take stock of and maximize the potential of all your available resources.
- **Fear:** Fear is a compass, a way to guide you toward personal growth.
- **Decisiveness:** You need quick decision-making skills to avoid complacency.
- **Speed:** You need to embrace failing fast for a rapid learning experience.
- **Tenacity:** You need to be constantly persistent to overcome challenges.
- **Ownership:** You need to take responsibility for all your actions.
- **Momentum:** Building a personal brand is difficult and requires momentum. Maintain daily engagement with your tribe.

I conclude by hammering home the importance of striving toward optimal outcomes, ensuring you maximize your time, prioritize productivity, and adopt a strategic mindset that will last you on your 90-day brand-building journey.

Free Chapter 3 Resources

I've designed a helpful guide to help you navigate this chapter's more in-depth and interactive secB tions. If you want to explore this in more detail, go to **dainwalker.com/resources/chpt3.** It's totally free, so make sure you don't miss out. You can also scan the QR code to get access.

SCAN ME

Chapter 4

SCOUT INDUSTRIES, MODEL PEOPLE

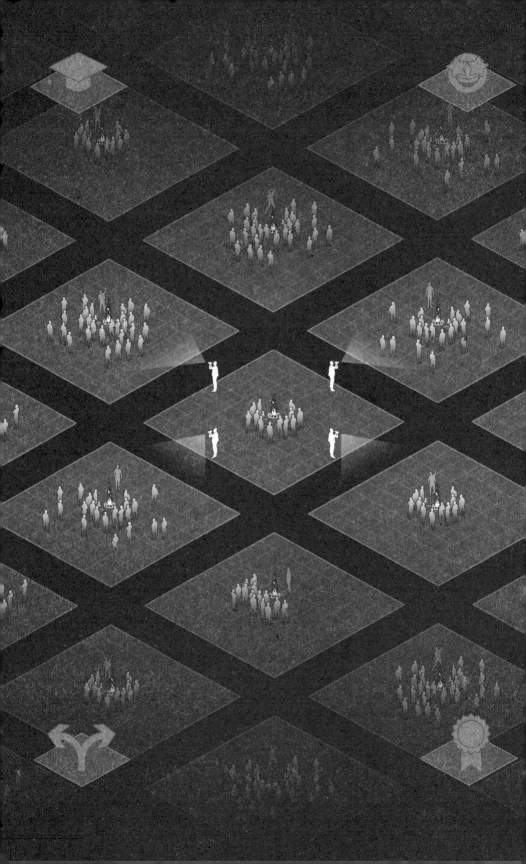

One night just prior to starting my content-creation journey, I sat staring at my computer late into the night. I knew I wanted to start posting content on my social feed, but what about? I was completely unsure of where to start, what to talk about, or what my content would even look like. I had no sense of niche, no frame of reference, or anything.

While I stared at my screen, the following questions went through my head:

- *What platform do I choose?*
- *How many platforms should I post on?*
- *How often should I post?*
- *What time of the day should I post?*
- *What should I post about?*
- *I'm not an expert at anything, so what should I talk about?*
- *Should I pick just one thing?*
- *How will I know if I picked the right thing?*
- *How will I know if it's any good?*
- *How much time will this take?*
- *Will I even be able to monetize it?*
- *What if I change my mind on what I want to do?*
- *What will my friends, family, and clients think of me?*
- *Will people think I'm a fraud?*
- *What if I fail and look like an idiot?*
- *What if I regret doing all of this?*

My point is, if any of this is familiar to you, you're not alone. I spent plenty of time feeling overwhelmed and stuck. But then Elli suggested I model my future content on work I admire and respect. Why shouldn't I look for inspiration in people who were already successful? This meant I had to create a model of others to follow.

Modeling others will serve you wonderfully as you grow your brand. As trends shift, modeling will help you adjust. As the algorithms (praise be the algorithm) change, modeling will help you stay relevant, and as industries evolve, modeling will help you evolve with it.

Okay, so, what do I mean by all that? If you look at your industry or niche like a chessboard, then doesn't it make sense to look at all the competitive pieces on the board?

Study Like a Student

The idea of modeling is to seek out the personal brand social accounts of the experts, thought leaders, educators, entertainers, and so on in your industry. Then carefully study what they do and how they do it, down to the minute details. You don't need to love everything they do; just study what they're doing. You might choose to model a small portion of what they do and leave the rest. The point is to scout out your industry to become deeply acquainted with the landscape and with what works in that landscape by observing other campfires.

Modeling others isn't just helpful as inspiration; by studying what works well for others and attempting to try it for yourself, you can also drastically accelerate the learning curve of becoming a content creator. Think of all the things others do with their content, such as how they speak, their design style, how they write, the format of their content, the topics they focus on, the type of audience they appeal to, how they speak about and solve problems, their humor, their personality, their setup, their editing style, and so on. Once you identify what parts of other personal brands you wish to model, you can adapt, change, manipulate, and combine these aspects with other things to create something that totally works for you.

Note, modeling is not stealing. It's studying something worthy of imitation, studying someone you admire whose actions and behaviors you find inspiring—some enough to adopt into your very own character. Modeling is experimenting with all forms of things that represent an inspirational ideal. Modeling is also how humans—and other primates—learn; we've spent our entire lives modeling family, friends, and colleagues, often unconsciously. What I'm talking about here is simply consciously modeling others so you can better understand the keys of their success and apply them to yourself.

One caveat: it's crucial that you don't fixate on one individual and copy everything they do. Take your time to find a handful of people to model. To keep it easy for myself, when I started producing content I modeled five people. Over time I kept adding people who inspired me, eventually learning from a lot of people—constantly trying on new things and attempting different techniques. This steady, curious student mindset kept me nimble, kept me relevant, and kept me pushing myself to become more.

 # Model the Greats

Initially like a student, I modeled constantly (and still do). Over time, from implementing all this modeling, I started to produce my own style and find my own voice. I was able to intuitively conceptualize my very own methods. I slowly curated how I spoke. I constantly challenged how I designed myself. I reviewed my delivery and whether it resonated or could be improved on. Modeling others in the early stages helped me gain momentum and altitude. By accumulating and duplicating what worked wonderfully for others, I was able to develop myself into what I do now as a personal brand. Through modeling others, I found myself, one piece at a time.

As mentioned, modeling can be a lot of things:

How someone speaks, their pace, and tone of voice: Modeling someone else's voice isn't about being inauthentic; it's about developing a speaking style that resonates with you and your personality. All famous orators study others' speaking styles. They observe the dialect, tone of voice, and pace at which they speak and pause—the highs and lows and inflections of their voices. They study the vocabulary used, and so on.

You'll probably not be surprised to learn that early on I modeled Gary Vee. I love his candid nature and how he speaks with so much power, conviction, and certainty. I love how he keeps his language very simple and brief. His tone and presence make him very relatable and down-to-earth. I enjoy how he uses humor to break the ice on difficult topics, and he isn't afraid to cut straight to the heart of a problem with someone right in front of him. He is opinionated, he is brash, he is full of energy, and he holds passion and enthusiasm in his voice. Gary can be a little polarizing, and I love that about him. Not everyone loves him, but the people who do feel relevant to me.

I was fascinated with how Gary can emotionally move an audience from the stage, so I studied his phrasings, his delivery, his pauses, and even his facial expressions (yes, I'm a nerd).

Studying Gary taught me to be more comfortable on the fly, to explore more candid, documentary-style content, and to just turn on a camera and go for it. He has the ability to make incredible content out of conversation, which has served me amazingly well when interviewing people on my podcast.

Gestures and body language: For those of you who wish to speak publicly or even film yourself for content creation, gestures and body language can say a lot about you. Your posture and eye contact can convey confidence. Your hand gestures can aid in your storytelling. When your gestures and vocabulary enrich your delivery, people will connect better with your content. For example, my team at Rivyl and I have studied the videos of me giving talks that we've posted online. We noticed that the videos in which I used great gestures and had good body language garnered more views than the videos when I wasn't quite on my game. Although this might sound like a small detail, a speaker's body language tells you a lot about them—and can make watching them all the more interesting.

I also loved studying Vinh Giang, someone I now call a friend but whom I once observed only virtually. His gestures are simple, powerful, and support his voice. His gestures invite me to listen, and keep me incredibly engaged. They emphasize his points, and train my eye to look at what he wants me to see. His gestures communicate a punchline or emphasize a phrase or statement. I find how he leans in, holds his hand up to his mouth, and whispers particularly captivating. Vinh is a magician, a wonderful orator and globally sought-after keynote speaker. All his gestures are on point, and I study him to this day.

In fact, Vinh is the reason I feel so confident on stage in front of thousands of people. I took inspiration from the level of effort and rehearsal Vinh puts into his preparation. How he uses his gestures to anchor an audience, to lead them visually, to keep them captivated and immersed are all techniques I've melded into my stage presence, and they've served me incredibly well (like I said, I'm a nerd).

Overall presentation: How someone presents themselves isn't just about the words they say and how they say them. There are many details involved in creating potent visual brand messaging in all formats, from the backgrounds of filmed content to lighting to the editing style of videos to the illustration styles of visuals that augment the content.

I've long appreciated Chris Do's overall presentation. Expensive microphones, lighting, and soundproofing in his spaces ensure that his audio and video are clear and effective. I also find his sense of fashion visually stunning; his wonderfully curated outfits, hats, accessories, and so on enrich his content so much. So, I've put a lot of thought to my own sense of fashion, lighting, backgrounds, and audio quality. Chris inspires me to pay close attention to details.

Embrace Adaptability

To recap a bit: from the very beginning of my journey, I constantly learned from others, picking up bits and pieces that I liked from everyone I observed. I became a student of others' styles, adopting pieces of many people. But—I didn't mimic each detail that inspired me; I morphed each detail into my own style and my own technique. What started as modeling melded into a unique form of its own.

Building a personal brand isn't about blending in, looking like everyone else. You want to be different from everyone else—drastically different. You don't want to be ordinary; you want to be extraordinary. This is why you must model first—and then master yourself second. After you've spent time studying and attempting to use the methods that work for others, you'll want to slowly adopt different techniques, continually evolving yourself well beyond your first 90 days.

Plus, when you remind yourself that crafting your brand takes time, the pressure eases, freeing you to explore many different things.

In other words: even once you find a recipe that works, don't get stuck relying on it. Instead, keep studying what others are doing: constantly seek new people to learn from and angles to add to your repertoire. Social media platforms change all the time. Algorithms (praise be the algorithm) shift, new features are introduced, trends come and go—and audiences get tired of seeing the same thing over and over again. Become a master.

Here's something I do with my personal brand. I scroll through my feed of the previous 30 days to see if I can detect transformation and improvement in my delivery, style, and technique. If I don't, I push myself to explore and experiment with new angles. So shake things up—keep your content diverse by constantly adopting and implementing new things.

But you know what? You don't have to take my word for it. Everyone you might be inspired to model got their start modeling the people *they* found inspiring. I know this because I've asked some of the people I've modeled, and they all shared that this process was part of their journey. I encourage you to do the same with your personal brand.

Exercise: Model Like a Nerd

1. Explore your terrain to seek out at least five people who inspire you—enough to want to model them. You might even find inspiration in people who aren't in your industry or niche. List those people in the following table.
2. Next, identify precisely what it is that you admire in each person, and consider which of those things you'd like to try on—and which don't work for you. Add those to the list.

The purpose of this exercise is to give you a baseline to start from. It's easier that you begin by modeling others than to start with nothing. By modeling others, their actions, and behaviors, and trying them on yourself like an outfit, you will more rapidly grow to understand what feels native to you. What feels natural to you, and what does and does not work for you. By modeling others, you can accelerate the growth of your content creation by constantly seeking to learn from others and what they're doing.

In any case, someone you are interested in might have traits, behaviors, and demeanors that you desire to model, but they might also simultaneously present themselves in a way that you either don't agree with or don't relate to. In this case, you can take the good and leave the bad, as you're just trying on the things that inspire you.

As an example answer: I like how certain presenters don't feel rehearsed, but I always like to have keynote slide decks and visual examples. It's about taking the feeling that it's unrehearsed and delivering that on stage with preprepared, supportive material.

Name	What you will model	What you will ignore
	• • •	• • •
	• • •	• • •
	• • •	• • •
	• • •	• • •
	• • •	• • •
	• • •	• • •
	• • •	• • •

Chapter Summary

I open this chapter by sharing my initial experience of feeling overwhelmed and stuck before finally starting and monetizing my content creation journey. I highlight many questions that I had for myself, and the doubts that arose when venturing into social media. These eventually disappeared with time.

This is done by a process I call *modeling*. You can do this by studying successful people in your industry whom you look up to. By approaching your business life like a student, you can carefully observe experts, thought leaders, educators, and entertainers in your field to see how they navigate their markets and provide for their tribes. You should pay close attention to speaking styles, body language, and overall presentation when performing a successful model.

I continue by emphasizing and reiterating that modeling is not copying; it's learning. It's a conscious effort that you make to truly understand the key aspects that make up a successful thought leader's journey. You shouldn't focus on one person. Diversify your focus and make sure you're getting everything you need from as many people as you need.

For me, this happened with several people. I modeled Gary Vee's candid nature, Vinh Giang's gestures and body language, and Chris Do's overall presentation. The important thing to remember here is that adaptability is paramount. It enables continuous learning and experimentation. I constantly advocate that you regularly evaluate and reevaluate your content to ensure you're always evolving.

Free Chapter 4 Resources

I've designed a helpful guide to help you navigate this chapter's more in-depth and interactive secB tions. If you want to explore this in more detail, go to **dainwalker.com/resources/chpt4**. It's totally free, so make sure you don't miss out. You can also scan the QR code to get access.

SCAN ME

GET
GOOD
THROWING
WOOD

So, back to the campfire. Now that we've covered prepping for surviving these 90 days and scouting and modeling aspects of your personal brand, it's time to start creating content. Because that's an enormous topic in and of itself, I've spread it out over two chapters. This chapter covers more of what needs to be done and when, in both the short term and long term. First up: attracting and retaining your audience.

Maintain Your Messaging

KEEP ADDING LOGS TO THE FIRE—NO MATTER WHAT. For example, if your campfire is the social media presence of your personal brand, then each piece of content you produce equates to another log thrown on the fire. Something I always remind myself is that, no matter how good a piece of content is, it's got a limited life span before it burns out and collects dust. On the plus side, the algorithm (praise be the algorithm) is often quickly done with content and ready to showcase new content, so don't worry if you post something and don't feel great about it. Post it anyway and move on. The point is to not overthink or overengineer each piece of content. It's more important to your tribe that you keep the flames red-hot by consistently throwing logs on your campfire.

Conversely, if you let the fire subside by not frequently adding more logs, it won't just deter your tribe from checking your page—it also sends a powerful negative message: that content is not your priority. In other words: you don't have anything to offer. If you post fresh content frequently, people imagine you're doing well; if you show up strong and consistently, many won't be able to fathom how you do it. People care way more about you showing up than how many likes your video gets. It's about consistency, not how popular you may seem. Seriously: even a tired, unloved post on your end will inspire support from your most devoted fans. The tribe you want to invest in the most is those who are invested in you the most. Be consistent and show up for them.

KEEP ON POINT. It's worth repeating: it's better to frequently post content that's average than to irregularly post content that's masterful. But be careful, because there's a balance to this. The goal is to not just haphazardly post about anything and everything. Part of establishing your personal brand is to clarify for your audience what your brand actually is—what you actually think and feel and believe and do. Keep consistently throwing content out there, and keep it on point.

Weather the Seasons

As long as we stay on a particular social media platform, we will be at the whim of the algorithm (praise be the algorithm). No matter what you do, platforms are going to be as unpredictable as the weather. One moment you're on top, growing your tribe rapidly—then suddenly everything's drying up and nothing seems to be working. This is precisely why consistency is important. What's also important as a content creator is that you don't get stale—it's crucial that you know what season you're in and how to make the most out of each one.

Winter

When the down periods arrive on social media, they don't just arrive for your campfire—they hit everyone in the marketplace like a strong, unfavorable winter. Even the most successful personal brands suffer under these conditions. Winter on social media is when, for whatever reason, the powers that be have adjusted their algorithm (praise be the algorithm) to be less favorable to a feature you're using (whether that content is text, graphics, audio, video, and so on).

It's precisely when these winters arrive and the weather's extra cold that you want to double down on posting content. This is when I post two or even three times more than usual. Why? Because while you're keeping your campfire as hot and as consistent as possible, your competitors are slowing down because of the cold—which just makes you burn all the brighter in comparison.

Now here's what I see happen all too often. A winter spell arrives, and your peers reduce their content production like they're going into hibernation. What's the point if they won't get as much reward for each output?

Better to conserve their resources, right? But when their campfire goes cold, their biggest fans—the most dedicated followers in their tribe—start wandering off into the wilderness seeking the warmth of someone else's campfire.

You see, if your audience isn't at your campfire, they're interested in someone else. They're at someone else's campfire, roasting marshmallows, creating fond memories with them, and considering committing themselves even further, buying their courses or products instead of yours. If you slow down you risk your appeal going cold—which could be just one step away from tribe members forgetting why you were once worthy of their attention. Even the most dedicated tribe member, the ones who seek you out every day, can get disheartened and look for their dose of dopamine elsewhere. So whatever you do, keep throwing wood on the fire: whatever logs, branches, or even twigs that will keep your campfire red hot.

Spring

Fortunately, every winter is followed by spring, which is all about new beginnings. When things start to take off again. It's a period of growth and acceleration that needs to be taken advantage of. This is usually when platforms introduce new features. When your platform presents you with a spring, that's the time to experiment, shake things up, test new ideas, and break the mold. Spring is the season of planting, and planting never produces immediate results. You need to invest in these new features before others do. Don't wait to see how to follow a trend; adopt new ideas early and plant your seeds first. If you have trouble doing this at first, model other campfires that have succeeded in this endeavor.

The best content creators know this, which is why you see them creating new forms of content every few months or so. So pay attention when the social media springs begin. Take advantage and plant your seeds; you'll certainly collect when it comes time to harvest.

Summer

Summer on social media is the good times. This is the golden sprint where everything you post is performing, your tribe is growing, your leads are piling in, and you're just in the zone, producing eye-watering slammers back-to-back. In the summer, just like in the winter, you want to double down.

Summers are when you've found formats that are bringing in new tribe members and converting them rapidly to paying customers. This means you want to stock the coffers and sell extra hard; you want to leverage your summers to stockpile enough to survive the winters. I've seen countless content creators take it easy when things are going great and then returning to find themselves in a winter, starving for leads, starving for growth, and struggling to keep up. You want to use the good seasons to get you through the tough ones.

Fall

The fall season is when you can tell that your content is slowly waning, declining in engagement and leads. When this happens, don't wait, don't complain. It's time to innovate. It's time to scout out what some of the latest trends are and find ways to implement them into your feed. It's time to give your tribe a shake-up. It's time to announce some extra freebies, drop a podcast, or make a free offer such as a webinar. Be extra creative to reward your tribe for sticking around for all four seasons.

On social media, the same weather hits us all. It's what we do to adapt to it that matters. If you don't adapt to the weather you're in, your page can die. If you get stale, get stagnant, get stuck; if you stop experimenting— then the winter will brutally punish you. However, if you plan ahead and work with the seasons, you'll be in better form to weather the harsh periods. Fortunately, the more seasons you go through, the better you'll get at predicting the weather and looking for signs of change. Social media is an extremely volatile place, with companies wrestling each other for the territory of consumer attention. Don't attach to it. Focus on what you need to do to build and maintain your campfire all year round.

 ## Build Your Tribe

So, how can you turn your efforts into income? Broadly speaking, if you encounter successful personal brands in your niche that are actively monetized, then there's a good sign that your space can be monetized. If you can position yourself at a similar pedigree, then people will be willing to pay you for your services, too.

If others have a significant growing tribe in a space, then so can you. What's important is that you identify who's offering alternative solutions to a problem a tribe is having. This is how you find your own voice.

What Makes Your Tribe Valuable

If someone's giving you precious minutes of their day to consume something you've created, that's incredibly valuable. But how can you use it? What can a tribe member give you?

- **Attention:** You can sell the amount of attention you have to sponsors in exchange for talking about their products or services.
- **Advocation:** Fans will feature you on their feeds and tell their friends about you.
- **Engagement:** Another metric you can sell to sponsors is how strong your community engagement is. Engagement is massive. You can use this to talk to your tribe, collecting insights regarding what they hate, what they love, what they want less of, and what they want more of. Engagement enables you to boost your content to perform better in the algorithm (praise be the algorithm). If you have tribe members who religiously comment, ask questions, and support you, then this is worth a lot. The higher your engagement rate is on any given platform, the more that platform is likely to push your content in front of strangers.

So, how can you take advantage of attention, advocacy, and engagement? You can easily build a base at the very outset of your journey:

1. Go to the pages of the people you're actively modeling and have similar tribes to you.
2. Click on their content.
3. Go to their comments section and start asking their followers questions.

4. When followers respond, reply with an insightful comment about their comment.
5. Then, shoot them a DM (direct message) and compliment them on their own content.

If you do this for 20 minutes and then you post from your own page, all those notifications will display on those strangers' phones. They will check out your page, and some will even give you a follow. More important, some will comment on your content. All this extra engagement will give the new post you potentially worked hours on curating a much higher chance of performing well.

This is what I call *campfire crashing*: proactively crashing, as much as possible, the comment section of all those who post content similar to yours. When I first started posting content in 2019, I would spend two to three hours per day campfire crashing. And even though my page had only 8,000 followers at the time, I could get 300 to 400 comments per post. If you go all out doing this, it's a powerful way to get your content train to leave the station. It's tedious, laborious, painstaking work, but if you stack all this activity over 90 days, you're going to get some seriously good results.

Attention, advocacy, and engagement aren't going to simply be handed to you. You need to earn it, you need to work for it, and you need to cultivate and provoke it.

How Your Tribe Engages with Your Campfire

In the same way that I recommend you analyze the terrain of your chosen niche, you'll want to have a strong sense of how your tribe members experience your content. In my experience, people tend to indulge, remember, process, and draw meaning from educational or entertaining content in one of three ways:

READING (diagrams, breakdowns, checklists, to-do lists, captions, emails, blogs, ebooks, books, etc.):
    Written content is still a potent format for delivering a message (such as this book). Plus, if the content is intended for an international audience, it can sometimes be easier for non-native speakers to read your

content than to listen to it. So it's crucial you include closed captioning/ subtitles of the spoken audio on your videos, and that you write content-rich captions that expand on whatever you're talking about in your post. The supportive copy could even be the reason your post goes viral; this has happened to me many times. Other forms of written content include a weekly newsletter for your brand and short ebooks you sell for a small fee or even give away for free. Of course, you can produce books like the one you're reading now. Most of the content I've included in this book is material I've worked on for years—crafting, testing, and experimenting every which way. My social media page is my biggest journal of all.

LOOKING (diagrams, photography style, filters, outfits, makeup, hair, accessories, backgrounds, transitions, demonstrations, fonts, colors, shapes, textures, elements, etc.): Some people are extremely visual, so it's important to keep that in mind when creating content. Experiment with adding a visual element or theme to your content. But don't just slap on some image or random photograph; if the visuals you choose don't resonate with your content, your tribe might have trouble understanding your message, no matter how well crafted it might be. I encourage you to take the same level of care with your visual content that you take with your written content.

LISTENING (podcasts, soundbites, webinars, audio books, audio courses, music, meditation, etc.): Audio is one of my favorite ways of taking in information. I'm often in transit: running between meetings, walking, doing chores, or working in the yard. It suits me because I can do other things at the same time as I'm learning. Audio is also how a lot of extremely successful and hyperbusy entrepreneurs like to consume content.

So, when you start progressing into the monetization phase of your brand, it's important to consider how you can best provide ways for your tribe to listen to your content in longer formats.

I initially underestimated the potency and value of audio content for the first few years of building my personal brand. It's also true that doing it well requires some time of investment—but for me the benefits have far outweighed the effort. Even if you're not ready to launch with this format, start saving material now to serve audio-loving tribe members in the future.

Cater to Your Tribe

Another consideration regarding how different tribe members choose to consume your content is how much they can take in in any one sitting—from a nibble to a snack to a full meal to an entire feast. So, let's return to the campfire framework and the metaphor of content being wood for the fire. In order to maximize the growth and reach of your page, you'll want to ensure that you package your content in various quantities—so all visitors can partake and leave satisfied.

Woodchips: Woodchips are small pieces of content—like a photo, a quote, or a short anecdote—something that's super quick and easy for the people who like to nibble to consume, save, and share with their contacts.

Because woodchip content is a great way to get people to feel more connected with you, it's smart to post woodchips frequently. In particular, snippets of stories—often about yourself—can effectively engage people who haven't yet been enticed to listen to or view your longer content. This is because humans are hardwired to be drawn to stories. Stories are definitely how I create the most engagement for my social channels.

I recommend posting woodchip content as frequently as possible throughout the day. People love to see what you do in life behind the scenes. They love hearing your raw thoughts, seeing more of the human side of you fleshed out. People will comment on your stories, start DM conversations with you, and even reshare your stories in their own stories, adding their own comments.

Because woodchip content burns fast, it's not as valuable as longer content, but you can still go viral with it, even without trying to. It keeps your personal brand top of mind. So if a nibbler visitor is considering hiring you or purchasing from you, seeing your woodchips might be that extra savory piece of content they needed to decide to commit.

Twigs: Twigs are for the people who snack. In my experience, the people who love twigs are those who doomscroll from post to post in search of that next hit of dopamine or serotonin. They want short-form content: items they can consume in 30 seconds during work breaks, on commutes, before crawling out of bed, or even sitting in bed for an evening stroll down Doomscroll Avenue. Many people with demanding schedules, lifestyles, kids, and such don't have time for much more than twigs, so it's smart to ensure you offer twigs aplenty.

Twig content could be a short entertainment skit to make someone laugh, an anecdote that's easy to relate to, or a lesson that's readily understood. Twig content shouldn't request much from the visitor.

Keep in mind to make your twig content clear, snappy, and quick, with a nice emotional payoff of some kind. Just a little something that's intriguing enough to enjoy briefly and then share with a fellow snacker.

Logs: Logs are for the people who enjoy consuming entire meals when they choose to visit your campfire—the content that's a little longer, a little deeper, and requires a little more of a commitment from the viewer. So this could be 90-plus-second videos, in-depth swipeable visual content, or text that isn't limited by word count.

This content is the stuff that burns a little longer on your campfire because it inspires a stronger volume of engagement, which is the secret sauce to gaining growth on any platform. So this is where you'll want to focus the core of your content creation daily for your first 90 days. Spend your time experimenting with ideas so you can get comfortable with regularly producing meal-length content.

Generally speaking, you want to focus on woodchips, twigs, and logs while you're still establishing yourself and figuring out how you want to position your brand.

Woodpile: Woodpiles are for the people who come to feast on offerings such as 20+ minute YouTube videos, podcast episodes, filmed webinars, or live performances. Once you've matured your personal brand beyond the initial 90-day sprint, start planning more big-form, slow-burning content. (I recommend you wait because woodpiles often have greater setup costs for equipment, set creation, and so on.)

Woodpile content is essentially compiling 20 one-minute valuable logs, for example, into one big piece of content. You can do this by recycling your most popular logs into one long format piece of content or expanding on one single log for as long as you see fit, such as this book (which is a forest of logs!).

The best thing about long-form content is the depth of immersion that it offers your visitors. In spending a length of time in your realm, people are more likely to feel connected to you, like you're a virtual mentor or someone they'd like to befriend. The longer someone spends with your personal brand, the more valuable that equity is to you.

Woodpile content should always be on the horizon—something that you're constantly working toward. The biggest, most heavily monetized personal brands on the internet have all figured out how to leverage long-form content to establish themselves as thought leaders, generally speaking.

Exercise: Carve Out a Wood Pile

Now that you've gotten a sense of the array of content you can offer, jot down ideas for text, visual, and audio content in the four quantities discussed in the last section.

The goal of this exercise is to understand that content creation comes in many forms and sizes, some of which are quick and snackable, and others require you to go more in depth and into the details than others. The smallest is the most digestible and easy to consume, and the largest are things you can comprehensively deep dive into.

Your logs are where you want to prioritize 80% of your attention in the first 90 days because this will represent the core fuel for your campfire. The twigs and wood chips enable you to give variety to those that don't have the time to spend long periods of time on your content. It's about making sure you're top of mind for as many tribe members as possible, as frequently as possible. For the exclusive tribe members who want to deep dive with you, they'll desire greater heat and value from the content you create, such as your woodpiles.

The agreement you need to make with yourself here is to continue to add as much wood as possible despite the weather and circumstances you may encounter. It's about being as consistent and plentiful as you can, to the best of your capabilities, as possible. This will keep your tribe warm and engaged at all times.

	TEXT	VISUAL	AUDIO
Chips	• • • • • •	• • • • • •	• • • • • •
Twigs	• • • • • •	• • • • • •	• • • • • •
Logs	• • • • • •	• • • • • •	• • • • • •
Woodpiles	• • • • • •	• • • • • •	• • • • • •

Chapter Summary

In this chapter, the focus is on content creation and building a loyal audience. The metaphor of a campfire is used to illustrate the dynamics of maintaining an engaging personal brand.

This chapter focuses on content creation and building a loyal tribe. I use the campfire analogy to drive home the point that personal branding is a multifaceted journey. It's a journey that I break down into several key factors:

Maintain Your Messaging

- Posting consistently is like throwing logs on your campfire. You need to do it with discipline without making excuses.
- You also need to acknowledge the power of the algorithm (praise be the algorithm) and try not to overthink your content.

Weather the Seasons

- Social media platforms can be thought of as operating in seasons, from the colds of winter, to the times of growth in spring, to the peaks of summer, and then to the steady yet manageable decline of fall.
- These are the times that you need to plan for accordingly to ensure that you don't fall behind your competitors.

Build Your Tribe and Cater to Your Tribe

- Success comes with effective monetization, and this comes by identifying your niche and how it can serve your potential tribe. It's about positioning yourself effectively in these parameters.
- The value of a tribe can be assessed in terms of how they give you attention, advocation, and engagement. The more you cater to these, the more fruitful your relationship will become.
- You can leverage the tribe of other people by performing what I call *campfire crashing*. This is a method by which you go to other tribes and cater to their needs on other territory.

Add Wood to Your Campfire
- Different content formats can be thought of as different types of wood, going from the smallest and most regular, to the largest and most involved: wood chips, twigs, logs, and woodpiles.
- Throwing these different pieces of wood on the campfire will ensure that you're catering to every level in your tribe. It maximizes audience engagement.

The overall point of the chapter is to ensure you adapt to the dynamic nature of social media and consistently provide content to diversify your offering and chances for success. It's ultimately about attracting the right crowd to create the right tribe for your personal brand.

Free Chapter 5 Resources

I've designed a helpful guide to help you navigate this chapter's more in-depth and interactive secB tions. If you want to explore this in more detail, go to **dainwalker.com/resources/chpt5.** It's totally free, so make sure you don't miss out. You can also scan the QR code to get access.

SCAN ME

Chapter 6

MASTER THE SMOKE SIGNALS

Theere are three additional approaches I use when creating content. All three include some aspect of identifying what might work, and then clarifying and solidifying what does work.

Work Five Themes

Two of the most important aspects of building a brand are clarifying what you are and broadcasting that with clarity. Think about it: how many vague, hazy brands do you remember? The problem with unclear brands is that people don't know how to think of them. In this example, they won't know who to think of you as, and so they won't know how to remember you. Many will drop out at this juncture. The more generous, curious types will ask you to clarify your brand for them. This means they have to use extra brain power to figure out what to think of you—whereas your goal is to have your personal brand land in their minds within the first five seconds of discovering you.

Learning how to create strong, effective content is a process. When you're still getting the hang of it, before you attempt to be clever with everything, focus first on being clear. Being clear in the first 90 days is much more important than being clever. Once you've mastered the art of being clear with your brand, you can give yourself the license to be more clever.

One way to learn if your content is clear enough is to note what questions people ask about your work. Let's say people ask, "So, what do you do exactly?" or "Can you explain what you do" or "Hey, how do you think you could help me?" If you're getting these questions, you're unclear. So, how can you present your personal brand so well it essentially smacks people in the face? Start by identifying your five key themes.

Where to Start

Your five key themes are the five primary things you will talk about for your first 90 days. Why five? I like to keep things simple. (Also, it's easier for brains to focus on just three to five things at once.)

I'll use myself as an example. When I started posting on Instagram I was not talking about branding. My themes changed constantly for the first year or so, and there's no shame in that. They changed with time as I figured out my true passions. You can change your five key themes as often and as frequently as you wish. My only suggestion is that you know what they are at all times. This will help you to stay on track and pivot effectively when you need to.

So here are five reasons why you'll want to identify your five key themes:

- Having five themes keeps you focused on a set of topics.
- If you repeat topics, you gain a reputation as being well versed in those topics. This gives you expertise through repetition, discipline, and credibility.
- Having five themes gives you enough room to experiment without asking too much from your audience.
- Having just five themes is simple enough for everyone to follow and retain.
- Having five themes gives you a consistent mechanism by which to audit yourself.

These were the five themes I used when I first started:

- Mindset hacks
- Sales tips
- Time management
- Client-relations tips
- Behavior tips

These were the topics I posted about in my first 30 days, the topics that I was genuinely interested in. With this content I was able to experiment with some formats that I was curious about. I also generated a lot of lead enquiries, especially for one-on-one coaching services. And that's good stuff. But, what did I become known for when I was doing this? People weren't entirely sure, and justifiably so. I was too fuzzy and too ambiguous about what my objective was. I also realized I was too similar to other creators, without having my own take on my subject matter. It didn't feel unique or exciting—and it was definitely not what I wanted to pursue for my agency.

So, after those first 30 days, even though these five themes were growing my page, I decided to completely switch it up and experiment with something different. At this time I was also testing different fonts, designs, colors, textures, and styles with my visuals. My point is, I didn't have everything perfectly figured out in the beginning, and neither will you, which is totally okay. Focus on experimenting with your themes.

When to Pivot

At about day 30, I pivoted to this second series of five key themes:

- Content creation tips
- Graphic design tips
- Instagram insights
- Instagram tips
- Social media monetization tips

Like I said, I decided to pivot because I realized, in part from the questions people asked me, that I needed to get much more clear about what I wanted to do with my agency. I also needed to home in on what I was good at. Because I had experimented for the first 30 days with my content, I started to realize I was really good at design—as well as making content—for not only myself but for a few others, too.

So I started creating a perception that I was "the guy" who could solve all their Instagram content-creation needs. That rapidly became my niche, and I repeated these five themes so effectively that people started calling me "the Instagram guy." They started to recognize me for one thing that I could clearly own in their minds. They didn't have to wonder what I was providing. They knew because my five key themes made it apparent. At the time, I thought, "Great, this is perfect." I was ecstatic. I'd figured out my niche, and I'd started to monetize it.

But, eventually, being known as "the Instagram guy" became more of a hindrance than an advantage.

Pivot Till You Find It

So I switched to the five key themes I'm known for now:

* Corporate branding
* Personal branding
* Graphic design
* Business tactics
* Entrepreneurship

I made these changes because I was moving completely out of content creation and content management and into the world of branding. I wanted clients to connect and reach out to me to ask for branding services.

Despite the fact that I'd amassed a substantial tribe for content creation, I was fortunately able to update my brand identity and take everything in a new direction. I've kept these themes pretty much in lockstep ever since, which is what built my preferred reputation as "the brand guy." I was invited to podcasts, I was paid to conduct keynote presentations, and I was asked to collaborate with companies for sponsorships—all while becoming a world-renowned expert on all things branding. And this reputation is exactly why I was given the opportunity by Wiley to write this book for you.

In summary, the five key themes that you adhere to through your content creation will be what position you in your audience's minds. It's through relentless repetition and stoking the campfire that a personal brand is built. This is why consistency is such an important ingredient in building your personal brand identity: to clarify exactly who you are, why you exist, what you offer, and why they should connect with you.

Interestingly so, the five key themes I landed on were the five things that I found the most interesting. Therefore, over the duration of the two years my five key themes orbited around my five key interests. Your niche usually correlates with the five things that resonate the most with you personally. I realized that what makes your niche your niche is what you makes you you—your niche *is* you. For me, I'm obsessed with corporate and personal branding, design, business, and entrepreneurship. This makes my content consistent and aligned with my true passions. By being your true self, you'll never run out of ideas, because you're constantly working with things that matter the most to you.

Exercise: The Five Key Themes

For this exercise, write down the first five key themes you intend to post with for your content. They can be whatever you like. There's no right or wrong here, no silver bullet. The point of this exercise is to decide on the themes you wish to experiment with, then come back at any time and change them later.

Pick five key themes that relate to your personal brand:

Key Theme 1:

Key Theme 2:

Key Theme 3:

Key Theme 4:

Key Theme 5:

Once you've selected your first five key themes (your niche), you'll want to map out how you'll cycle through them over your first 30 days. So what you need to do is select your five key initial themes and cycle through them, like this:

- Monday post theme 1
- Tuesday post theme 2
- Wednesday post theme 3
- Thursday post theme 4
- Friday post theme 5
- Saturday post theme 1
- Sunday post theme 2
- And so on (*Rinse. Repeat.*)

And just to emphasize this before we move on: whatever five themes you pick to start with, whether you keep them for a month or a year, if you realize you've outgrown them, don't be afraid to pivot. Sometimes we have to do things we're unsure about to unearth the things we're completely sure about. It took me two years to figure out what I wanted my current niche to be—even more to understand what that truly meant. It meant being able to identify what made me me. That's my niche. Fortunately, whatever you build with one niche, you can pivot toward a new niche. Keep going until you truly understand your passions. Not every tribe member will come with you, but a significant portion will.

The reason you're doing this in rolling succession is so you can live test which of the five key themes is working and which is not. In any case, if you do this consecutively for 30 days, rolling the themes over and over again, you'll hit each theme six-plus times with your content.

Explore and Expand

Once you've selected the five key themes you're going to start with, you'll want to drum up content topics for your first month on social media feeds. The way I recommend proceeding is to come up with a slew of questions that a potential client might ask about any of your key themes. This calls for jotting down as many questions about each key theme that you can muster—and then answering them. For example:

- What exactly is it?
- How do I use it?
- Why is it important?
- What if I don't use it?
- What's the impact of it?

We'll flesh this out with one of my key themes: graphic design.

Q: **What exactly is graphic design?**
A: Graphic design is a visual communication tool for businesses.

Q: **How do I use graphic design?**
A: You use graphic design by creating a system/structure for your team to deploy.

Q: **Why is graphic design important?**
A: Graphic design is important because it will alter customer perception.

Q: **What if I don't use graphic design?**
A: If you don't use graphic design, then your company won't look cohesive, which will lose client trust.

Q: **What is the impact of graphic design?**
A: The impact of graphic design is the ability to increase the foreseen value of your product/service and charge more.

Ask yourself whatever questions you like, and provide as many answers for each question as you like. I recommend writing down 40 ideas for each theme. If you chose a good theme, this should not be too difficult to do. If it is difficult, I encourage you to swap it for a theme that's easier for you to talk about from your own expertise.

Once you've listed 40 ideas for each of the five themes, for a total of 200 ideas, then review all your ideas, one theme at a time, to identify which ideas speak to you the most. To keep this on your campfire, think about picking your five key themes like selecting the five types of wood you want to use in your campfire. Then, the process of breaking each theme into ideas for posts is the equivalent of chopping the wood into woodchips, twigs, logs, and woodpiles.

Go Viral

We humans are predictable creatures of habit, and there are specific things that social media experts, marketers, advertisers, and salespeople know that we can't help but respond to. These surefire approaches pretty much fall into six categories, and one or more of them are behind every meme, post, story, or report that's gone viral. Think of them like smoke signals that you send out to your tribe.

 Study the Six Smoke Signals

Once you become versed in these viral approaches, broadcasting these smoke signals to your tribe will go far in building your personal brand:

Evocative content—content that evokes **power, status, aspiration, and sex**—gets our attention because of our core biology. Essentially, those of our ancestors who had more power, status, and interest in sex—plus those who aspired toward those things—were far more likely to pass on their genes than those who weren't. And so we're naturally drawn toward anything that might advertise to others that we have status, significance, and sex appeal: like showing off wealth via a fancy car, a beautiful house, a luxury holiday; showing off a sexy body; or showing off the ability to buy or build what others could never achieve.

I'm personally more inclined to be very covert about these things, in part because this smoke signal can be seen as showboating, gloating, and boasting, which can be a turn-off for some audiences. But, nonetheless, what turns one audience off will attract another, and evocative content definitely attracts.

Reactive content is the **strange or bewildering** stuff capable of sparking curiosity or even a bit of confusion. This content draws our attention because the ancestors who took the time to try to identify or understand something new fared better than those who didn't.

Reactive content provokes a reaction; it makes you stop scrolling to scratch a sudden itch. It triggers fun and positive emotional reactions in most cases. If you can spark someone's curiosity and even confuse or bewilder them a little, you'll have their undivided attention.

Relative content is **familiar, nostalgic, or comforting**. It evokes feelings of connection, similarity, or likeness—like relating to an experience you've had or eliciting the comfort of feeling someone understands the world the way you do. These evocations derive directly from tribal identity: we tend to feel safest when among our "own kind."

In practice, this is the viral meme that makes you think, "That's so true; that's me" or "That's exactly what my friend does." A lot of people respond positively when I post snapshots of my life on my stories that they can relate to and share. When done right, content that's relative will attract and hold visitors' attention.

Provocative content elicits **tension**, even **shock**. It's the material that makes you feel uncomfortable, **provoking** a strong emotional reaction, such as to a moral dilemma or topic of debate. The most provocative material can even force us to question our belief systems or sensibilities—which really holds our attention. (Again, this effect derives from our sense of tribal identity; we are strongly disinclined to go against our established tribal culture.)

But provocative content doesn't have to be negative. It can be a fun, interesting spin on a serious or otherwise bland topic. I use provocative content all the time, for example, when you purposely try to spark a reaction through questioning a popular or commonly shared belief, such as an industry status quo.

Confronting content is the **scary or threatening** stuff that puts you on edge with a sense of **impending danger or risk**, perhaps eliciting a mild state of fight, flight, or freeze. Humans are hyper-attuned to anything that could be dangerous, so effectively using confronting content will inevitably garner a lot of attention. You'll unlikely not be surprised to hear that this sort of content is the most likely to go viral because our ancestors were prone to spreading the word if danger lurked around the corner.

Captivating content is the material that leaves you feeling **awe-inspired**, with a sense of **wonder** or **mystery**. This could be majestic scenery or an emotional, touching moment, or a tale of someone overcoming something against all odds.

Captivating content often goes viral because people love to share inspiring stuff with others—another nod to humans' attraction to story.

Master the Six Smoke Signals

Now that you have a sense of why different click-bait approaches can be effective, apply that knowledge to what you encounter in the wild. Pay close attention to what content is actually going viral, and identify why it earned that status. I promise you it will derive from one or more of the six smoke signals categories. Start becoming hyperaware of what viral smoke signals are being used by your competitors and those who inspire you. I've tested and experimented with all six of these over the past years, and my top-performing viral posts always include at least one or more in each post.

And when you're producing content, play with employing these smoke signals to give yourself the best reach and chance possible of going viral—while also simply learning what works with your audience. Like concocting a content cocktail, you can mix and match them together to create different reactions and see what works for you. Your first 90 days call for experimenting, having fun, taking risks, getting bolder, and seeing what interesting ideas you can stumble on in this playground of novelty.

 ## Grab and HOLD

Grab and HOLD is the final part of the process I use to create content. Everything I make for my content is engineered to take the viewer on a journey and give them a payoff at the end. This engineering involves separately taking each theme and filtering it through all four approaches of what I call the *HOLD method*: hook, own, love, and direct. These four methods will help you adjust your content to be as effective as possible:

H = Hook: You want to engineer absolutely every piece of content you create to have a solid emotional or logical hook in it—whether it involves power, shock, inspiration, mystery, or something else. This is because you need a strong hook to emotionally grip someone enough to switch from doomscrolling mode to engagement mode—with *your* content. You want to land them hook, line, and sinker. This is the first four seconds of a video, the appeal of upfront graphics, the soundbite that draws them in, the headline that demands further investigation.

If you want your campfire to outperform the other nearby campfires, you need to master this better than anyone. The goal here is to make it immediate.

O = Own: Once you've hooked your visitor, you want to "own" their desire for the payoff. This calls for holding something in reserve, baiting their attention until the end of the video or post with the promise of reward: a promised reveal, a promised solution, a promised scratch for their overwhelming itch.

This is what will make your content addictive. When you can master the ability to own someone's attention from beginning to end, you've mastered the theater of content creation. This isn't easy by any means—it will take practice to develop. But this "own" should always be your goal when creating content.

L = Leverage: Next, you want your visitor to distinctly love what you offer. You want your content to leverage the wants and needs of your audience to provoke a reaction. It's about enticing someone to engage with your personal brand, not just view the content and move on. You want them to genuinely engage, genuinely resonate with your energy, and genuinely respond with emotional connection. People love to love people; your objective is to develop content that triggers a reaction of some kind.

This is essentially a sense check, ensuring that every time you make a piece of content, you're actively checking whether it will resonate with your tribe. Is it something they need? Something they desire? Something that triggers a response of some kind?

D = Direct: Finally, don't have your piece of content drift off into nowhere. You need it to land on something solid. You need to reveal the solution, unveil the magic, and direct them to next steps—some form of call-to-action. In entertaining content this is the punchline, where you direct them to emotionally react, emotionally engage, and end the video or piece of content on a high. In more serious content, this principle remains the same; you just need to avoid drifting from the concept of the content itself.

When you can consistently perfect your content with the HOLD method, and hold someone's attention from front to end, your content will undoubtedly take off and your page will inevitably grow.

Exercise: Experiment Madly

What's my direct to you in this chapter? I want you to go out and experiment like a mad scientist. Your campfire is your domain, and you can do whatever the hell you want with it. What's important is that you make this process fun and experiential for *yourself*. This is important because if you're not having fun it will come through in your voice and in your body language.

So go have fun. Play with the different smoke signals to see what brings people to your campfire and HOLDs their attention. Simply fill in the blanks here and get started.

Be kind to yourself in this process. The first few may not be as perfect as you intend. This will get better with time.

Idea 1:	
H	*How will this post get attention? (e.g., evocative, reactive, relative, etc.)*
O	*What will this post promise as a reward? (e.g., solution, learning, insight, etc.)*
L	*How will this post leverage them to react? (e.g., like, comment, share, and save, etc.)*
D	*What action will this post direct them to do? (e.g., start a 90 day brand plan, etc.)*

Idea 2:	
H	*How will this post get attention? (e.g., evocative, reactive, relative, etc.)*
O	*What will this post promise as a reward? (e.g., solution, learning, insight, etc.)*
L	*How will this post leverage them to react? (e.g., like, comment, share, and save, etc.)*
D	*What action will this post direct them to do? (e.g., start a 90 day brand plan, etc.)*

Idea 3:	
H	*How will this post get attention? (e.g., evocative, reactive, relative, etc.)*
O	*What will this post promise as a reward? (e.g., solution, learning, insight, etc.)*
L	*How will this post leverage them to react? (e.g., like, comment, share, and save, etc.)*
D	*What action will this post direct them to do? (e.g., start a 90 day brand plan, etc.)*

Chapter Summary

In this chapter, I outline the strategic approach that I recommend for creating content on social media to effectively build a personal brand that knows its tribe. These key points include the following:

The Importance of Clarity in Branding
- To be clear is to make sure that your tribe even knows what you're talking about. Without clarity, no one will know what you're doing and what you're offering.
- Practicing clarity repetitively is the only way to ensure long-lasting success.
- Do this in 90 days to ensure maximum efficiency and learnings.

Adapting and Pivoting Themes
- When figuring out your five key themes, you need to have flexibility, ensuring that you give your space to evolve and grow over time.
- I offer some of my personal experiences, sharing how I struggled but eventually locked down the five key themes I still use today.

Understand Viral Content Strategies
- I outline the six smoke signals that need to be top of mind if you're interested in creating viral content: evocative, reactive, relative, provocative, confronting, and captivating content. I explore each in detail.
- These smoke signals need to be practiced consistently to be of any use.
- The HOLD method is a framework for content creation that can be broken down into four key elements:
  - **Hook:** You need to create a strong emotional or logical hook in the first few seconds of your content to keep readers engaged.
  - **Own:** You need to then keep the audience's attention, perhaps by promising them a reward or eventual payoff for sticking around.
  - **Leverage:** You need to target genuine audience engagement through emotional storytelling and authenticity.
  - **Direct:** You need to offer a clear call to action that directs your tribe to either pay for more services or engage with more of your content.

The key takeaway here it to keep experimenting to ensure you're never left wondering if you could've tried the right approach. Ultimately, to ensure the success of your personal brand, you need to make sure that you give yourself every chance to achieve that success. That is done through repetition and experimentation.

Free Chapter 6 Resources

I've designed a helpful guide to help you navigate this chapter's more in-depth and interactive secB tions. If you want to explore this in more detail, go to **dainwalker.com/resources/chpt6.** It's totally free, so make sure you don't miss out. You can also scan the QR code to get access.

Chapter 7

GIVE VALUE, EARN LOYALTY

The entire concept of building a personal brand is understanding that you're sharing your expertise, your value, and your credibility. But more than anything, building a personal brand is all about serving your tribe; it's about your ability to lead others—not your ability to promote yourself.

So many brands get this wrong when promoting themselves on social media. They often showcase how perfect they are, how wonderful their life is, and so on. But what's in it for the visitor? To truly master personal branding is to truly understand what exactly the visitor wants *from* you, what they would find valuable about you, and what use it is to them—essentially, to convert them from a visitor into a tribe member.

The process of building a tribe and earning their trust—and then developing products and monetizing your personal brand—is so intertwined that it's impossible to separate them out into distinct chapters. So though we'll generally proceed conveying the philosophy behind it all before turning to more tangible execution, there will be some echoes in the forecasting, and some follow-up before getting started.

Also, it's crucial that you have a very strong sense of all that needs to be done before a prospective tribe member gets a whiff of anything being sought from them. (Spoiler alert: no one should ever get a whiff that something will be requested of them—other than feedback.) So bear with me if you feel impatient. We'll get to the tangibles before long.

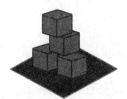 ## Build Your Tribe

Like I said, building a personal brand is all about building a tribe that you then serve; it's about your ability to lead others. It's also about your ability to demonstrate how much you have to offer, and why they should stick around.

Give Value, Earn Loyalty

Let's say the internet is a library, and your social media content is available on one of its shelves—jam-packed with all the insights and stories and knowledge you have to offer.

Now, when someone goes to a library, what are they looking for exactly? Well, one of three things:

Something to entertain them: fictional or factual journeys that essentially immerse the visitor in some form of experience

Something to inform them: anything tactical, functional, or practical that the visitor can use in some way, often for a specific purpose

Something to educate them: something to provide a broader understanding of one or more topics just for the sake of it, like this book

If you're producing content and putting it on the shelf, and you want someone to want to read it, you'll need to effectively and cleverly pick at least one of these three options. However, too many people don't do that. They focus on the sale, which is an immediate turnoff. (Remember my story in Chapter 2: Leave Your Comfort Zone about how different Gary Vee's approach was from the other speakers at that conference? I wrote, "All the other speakers produced content in order to sell something. But Gary didn't. He was only interested in helping his audience start their journey, whatever it was." He also started his talk with "Guess what?! I'm not here to sell you shit!")

Selling your products is like putting up a poster in the public library that reads: PLEASE BUY MY SHIT. Unless someone's a dedicated fan, they're not buying. The trouble is, once you've done this the audience will associate you and your brand as being about the sale and always trying to sell or pitch something—even if you think you're being covert about it. Something as simple as "come to my event" or "listen to my podcast" can be perceived by your visitor as hard selling.

Instead, I recommend behaving like an author. Each post you put up, each log on your campfire, is just another chapter in the endless book that is your social page. You're actively authoring your life—telling stories, sharing tips, and giving advice. The more valuable your content, the more your tribe think you're worth. The bigger your tribe grows, the more active the engagement, the more rapidly it happens. This adds value and credibility to your personal brand.

To grow a community you need to become a community leader. This is why it's crucial to be consistent and persistent with content production and with making yourself visible and available. Your community must see you as unshakable, ever-present, and a constant provider. And you'll do it for free—you'll do it for the love of providing. In return, ironically or not, you'll get more of what you want. The only way to get this outcome is by giving lavishly without expectation, by serving, and by being a leader that your community will respect and unite their belief system with.

Earn Every Plank

Each person who follows your page and sits around your campfire is unique, with no set bandwidth to offer. Just because you have followers doesn't give you the license to just start selling them anything. Preparing your tribe to spend money requires time—during which you'll want to be dedicated to providing value. There is no volume of boosting posts or paying for ads that can replace legitimate brand equity.

Your brand equity is the value each tribe member places on you and your personal brand. To a tribe member who's been engaging with your content daily for months, you may be worth a lot—and if you have a high brand equity in their mind, they might be likely to make a buying decision. This can't be said of someone who has spent less time at your campfire, generally speaking.

As a tribe leader, you need to cultivate and incubate how each person feels about you and your community. Your goal is to provide them with free value. The mantra of this game is "How can I out-provide (give more than) all my competitors?"

You can also think of this in terms of the levels of "fandom"—in which case the question is "How can I inspire people to go from being vaguely aware of my existence to being overjoyed that I exist?"

If your content were a campfire, then your brand equity would be the bridge someone needs to cross to develop from being vaguely aware to being infatuated with it. I think of the journey from one state to the other as being like crossing a bridge with seven planks:

- **Impartial:** They've noticed you, and heard of you, but they haven't made an effort to care for you or your brand.
- **Observant:** They care enough about you to actively check out your personal brand when their social media displays it to them.
- **Curious:** They're curious enough to try to better understand your brand—by deep diving through your content and browsing your links.
- **Engaged:** They're actively engaged with your brand; they go out of their way to find you and see what you've been up to. They'd also notice—and care—if you failed to make an appearance.
- **Enthralled:** They're more than engaged: they excitedly anticipate your content, they comment on almost everything, and they ask when your next products will appear.
- **Advocative:** They actively promote your brand, they endorse you, and they demand others follow you.
- **Addicted:** They buy everything you sell, they attend your events, and they advocate you constantly. They genuinely love you and what you do.

To build your tribe you need to encourage people to wholeheartedly cross that bridge and commit to becoming a full-blown tribe member of your personal brand. You do this by offering massive volumes of free content, as consistently as possible—woodchips, twigs, logs, woodpiles, logs, twigs, woodchip. Become more valuable; give away excellent content every single day. Give them your best secrets, your best insights, your best tips—absolutely everything.

It's common to think you should reserve your best material; what's uncommon is for you to give it all away. This will enable you to capture the maximum possible attention for your social page. Now, something else happens when compressing massive levels of energy into your first 90 days. Everyone near or on the bridge sees how others engage with your page, how fast your page is growing, and how frequently you post. All of this contributes to how quickly each person crosses your bridge.

Here are 11 ways you can offer your tribe constant value:

- Give them your expertise, in varied formats and quantities.
- Give them free downloadable ebooks.

- Give them exclusive access to your expertise. Allow them to ask you questions, to meet in person, to attend private events.
- Offer a giveaway of your services/products.
- Give them long-form podcasts of yourself teaching or interviewing guests.
- Give them live calls and interview guests to help them with things you don't teach elsewhere.
- Give them curated feed content (intentionally crafted and pre-audited content) to share with their communities.
- Give them behind-the-scenes content of your life and the process of what you do.
- Give them affiliate links so they can also monetize themselves off the courses you're selling, and so on.
- Give them exclusive access to a community group where you can have more of their attention off-platform.
- Give them encouragement; if you notice they're advocating for you, go out of your way to express your gratitude.

The idea here is you want to engage with your tribe members. Befriend them, and find new and creative ways to connect with them. Do whatever it takes to protect your tribe, to keep them well fed, and to give them as many tools as possible. This only adds fuel to the fire.

There's a law of reciprocity at work in this approach. What you give on social media you will get back. It will likely not be immediate, but it will be plentiful.

The Three Hurdles of Trust

I hope you're beginning to understand the complex nature of building a campfire, and why it takes time to master each of these elements: they're all intertwined, and they work off each other in the process of building your personal brand.

To earn your tribe members' trust enough for them to consider buying your goods or services, you must convince them of three essential aspects of your brand: they need to trust the WHO, the WHAT, and the HOW of you. In other words, they need to trust who you are, what you offer (and what of it is relevant to them), and how you will effectively provide it to them. For this you need to unwaveringly convey your credibility, your relevance, and your reliability—to essentially build three pillars of trust. To break this down into even smaller pieces, I'll also convey some of the who or what or why of each of these.

Build Your Credibility

The *what* of credibility: As stated previously, people trust people far more than they trust entities (such as companies). People would much rather consult with a human they already know about (and, ideally, follow) than with a company that targeted them via some form of marketing or ad campaign.

For someone to open their wallet, they must trust that there is a reason to spend precious resources. For someone to open their wallet to you, they must trust *you*. So the first thing you want a tribe member to trust is you—more than your product or service, and more than your process. Without that trust, the value of your offer is irrelevant. Without that trust, your braggadocious guarantee of the results you'll provide falls on deaf ears. You need your tribe to believe that you, and only you, are the person for the job.

The *how* of credibility: Because the very heart of your campfire is trust, the way you gain trust from your tribe and others is by being helpful to as many people as possible as frequently as possible. This is why you must keep your fire burning with the content creation you keep churning, because if your content slows down your fire will die down, and your enquiries will fade.

Showing up every day builds trust. Consistently offering high-value content builds trust. And giving away free content actually helps build trust. This trust, in my opinion, is far more important than any money your brand will make. Money can't incubate trust, but trust can definitely incubate money. Trust incubates opportunities, trust incubates enquiries, and trust can incubate referrals.

Your personal brand is an incubator of trust; the more trust you can build with your tribe, the more likely they'll be willing to make transactions with you. With every piece of content, with every one-on-one interaction, with every referral, you're essentially building an empire of trust. The bigger the reach your campfire has, the greater your capacity to talk to people one-on-one—and the greater your referrals will be. All of this combined produces the opportunities for you to monetize yourself.

So, when producing content as a personal brand, keep trust building at the very front of your mind at all times. With every log you throw on the campfire, ask yourself, "Will this help build trust in my tribe?" If the answer is yes, then power on!

Cultivate Your Relevance

The *what* of relevance: Once you've established the trust that you are valuable, knowledgeable, and endearing—and, thus, that your personal brand is to be trusted—then and only then will your tribe consider if they should trust what it is that you're offering. This is particularly pertinent in terms of if what you offer is relevant to them—if its inherent value (if it has any; they don't know yet) is valuable to them.

In Chapter 8: Find Cows, Cook Meat I talk about the product that you'll create as your meat: the logs on the campfire are the content that keeps your tribe warm; the meat on the fire is what some tribe members will decide to partake in. So think about this in culinary terms: if you go to a restaurant but then realize you don't trust the chef, you won't eat anything they make. Even once you trust the chef as a person, that doesn't mean you'll automatically trust what's on their menu. Even if you trust them implicitly as a person—let's say they're your best friend—you might still be reluctant to trust their professional acumen (especially if you've never seen them cook before). In other words, your product needs to be able to sell itself; it needs to earn its own trust.

Consider these types of client inquiries:

- Do you have experience working in this industry?
- Can you show me a successful case study of working with a client like me?
- Can you give me a guarantee that this is going to work?

If the tribe member/prospect asks questions like these about your product or service, congratulations: that means they have a degree of trust in you and your personal brand. You've passed the first hurdle. So now you've reached the second hurdle, because what they want to know at this stage is if you're up for the task. So how can you demonstrate that what you offer is relevant to them?

The *how* of relevance: To make your product or service relevant to the tribe, you need to fully understand what their needs are. Similarly, you must use communicative language about your product to ensure its merits are clear to everyone, phrased such that they will understand clearly. If they have a basic understanding of what you're offering, then you'll want to discuss it in a basic way. If they have an intermediate understanding of what you're offering, then you'll want to discuss it in an intermediate way. If they have an expert understanding of what you're offering, then you'll want to discuss it in an expert way.

Because of this, I strongly recommend that—at the very minimum—the first conversation you have with any prospective tribe member is a one-on-one and synchronous conversation, preferably via video (or in person) or via telephone. Ideally all such interactions would be both one-on-one and synchronous—so you can base the way you communicate your product offering on how you think it will be best received. If they speak like a beginner, match their language; if they speak like an expert, match their language.

Conveying information in a one-on-one conversation is your best opportunity for building trust for two reasons. First, we're simply hardwired to respond better to a live human than to boilerplate copy, and second, tailoring your responses to what the other person states they need enables you to specify exactly why and how your offering is relevant to them. Since the beginning and to this day, I've sold products exclusively through one-on-one conversation—unless the product was a course, book, event, or webinar. To sell my core service offering requires an in-depth conversation in which I can connect with the client and carefully explain exactly what my product is and why they need it—with my phrasing tailored for maximum comprehension. In the tribe's mind, relevance is everything; the best way to connect with relevance is always with a one-on-one conversation.

There's a deeper angle to this as well. Relevance is also a game of perception. Humans are more likely to trust people who are similar to them in as many ways as possible. (This derives from our ancestors being far more likely to trust only those in their tribe.) So if you're speaking with a business owner and they perceive you as being a beginner freelancer, they're less likely to trust what you say. Or let's say they're a start-up entrepreneur and you position yourself as the world's leading authority on a topic . . . you can also lose trust as they may feel intimidated working with you. Appearing like too much of an expert and too credible can make your brand appear irrelevant to them. This is why identifying your tribe is essential. Business owners prefer to do business with another business owner, whereas freelancers prefer to do business with freelancers, generally speaking.

You can earn a tribe member's trust by demonstrating that you are like them: of the same mind, of the same circumstance—of one accord. It's okay to be a few leaps beyond them or a few leaps behind, but the more you demonstrate how well you understand the world they're in and the problems they face, the more likely they will trust what you have to say. So, with your product or service, it's important to convey exactly how your offering will address the full spectrum of their problems. Don't promise too much; they might not need everything you're offering, so it won't feel like a perfect match. Similarly, don't offer too little, because that could suggest you're not capable of effectively solving their problem. Instead, clarify how your offering is their perfect match.

Establish Your Reliability

The *what* of reliability: The third important angle of encouraging your tribe to purchase what you offer concerns how you will deliver. Your objective is to develop their trust in your approach, your system, your follow-through. They want to know that the way you operate resonates with the way they conduct business.

So you'll want to clearly demonstrate that transacting with you will produce their desired outcome. You can do this by clarifying for them the entire path from A (the moment they sign the deal) to Z (the moment their desired outcome is complete). This is when all trust hurdles have been cleared.

The *how* of reliability: In the early days of monetizing my personal brand, I was able to convince clients that I was the right person for the job. I was able to convince them that what I offered was relevant to them. But my clients struggled to see *how* the plan would come together and *what* they'd be left managing at the end of it. This is because I hadn't yet realized the importance of this third trust hurdle, and so I hadn't thought to take the necessary steps.

But to attain maximum trust from my clients, I needed to not only listen to their problems and educate them on how I would solve them but also show them *how* I was going to produce their solution. Once I learned how to convey my unique approach and exactly how I would deliver, this last trust hurdle firmly supported the trust the client needed to feel, and I was able to increase my pricing. I did this by taking them on a visual journey—via a PowerPoint breakdown or simple PDF—mapping out all the stops they could expect on the way (just like I did with the trust hurdles). For example:

- **Step 1:** We're going to conduct a workshop with your team to identify precisely what your content needs to achieve.
- **Step 2:** With the information we learn from that workshop, our team will ideate possible content topics.

- **Step 3:** We'll then present these ideas to you for you to approve which you like.
- **Step 4:** We'll then design a mockup template of what your first nine pieces of content would look like.
- **Step 5:** We'll write captions for this content, which we'll submit for your approval.
- **Step 6:** We'll identify the most effective hashtags for your social page(s).
- **Step 7:** We'll schedule your first months' worth of content.
- **Step 8:** After the first month of content publication, we'll run an audit to gauge how effective it is.
- **Step 9:** Based on that analysis, we'll . . . (etc.).

To recap, the client needs to know the following information to trust working with you:

- Exactly what will be delivered
- When it will be delivered
- How they would need to be involved
- What I would need from them in order to fulfill the agreement

So, at the end of the day, establishing trust and nurturing genuine credibility are the two most important lingering effects of a successfully executed personal brand.

Exercise: Plot Out Your Content Value

In this exercise I want you to get clear on the value exchange between you and your tribe—what you're giving and what they're receiving. It's important that your branding is not only clever but also completely clear to your tribe as to what you're giving them.

Q: **What are you giving away? (what value)**
A: "I'm giving advice on how to decide on a name for a company."
Q: **Why should they care? (relevance to them)**
A: "It's relevant to start-ups as they always have naming challenges."
Q: **Why should they listen to you? (credibility)**
A: "I'm credible as I've named 100s of brands and I'm seen as a brand expert."

Simply write down as many valuable things you intend to give away, why each of them is relevant, and why they should trust you of all people to provide it. It's crucial with each piece of content you produce that you remind yourself that it must be clear what inherent value you're giving to the viewer.

What are you giving away?

Why should they care?

Why should they listen to you?

Chapter Summary

This chapter discusses seven key learnings, ranging from building the foundations of your personal brand to cultivating relevance and reliability within your tribe. They go as follows:

Foundations of Personal Branding
- Personal branding is essentially about sharing your expertise, value, and credibility.
- It's about ensuring your tribe gets something useful from you.
- You need to understand your tribe's needs to effectively create a desirable offering.

Building Your Tribe
- You need to consistently focus on demonstrating your value on social media to build an engaged tribe.
- Always be genuine. Don't try to oversell by pumping your tribe with sales pitches.
- Be consistent and persistent at all times.

Earning Trust and Brand Equity
- Trust comes about with credibility, relevance, and reliability.
- Building trust is a long journey that comes from awareness of your position in your market and your tribe's needs and wants within that market.

Offering Constant Value to Your Tribe
- I discuss that there are multiple ways to offer constant value for free, and that this is paramount when building and maintaining a tribe.
- You need to constantly engage your tribe and respect the trust they put in you.
- By providing this value, you're opening up the door for your tribe to pay you back with attention, engagement, and more.

The Three Hurdles of Trust
- Your tribe needs to get past the three hurdles of trust: trusting you as a person, trusting your product, and trusting your process.

- Keeping your tribe engaged in the long term is more important that immediate monetary gains.

Cultivating Relevance
- You need to also internalize your trust.
- Trust your product, and relevance will come.
- Staying relevant is crucial to your long-term success as a personal brand. This fire needs to be constantly stoked.

The Reliability of Your Process
- Visualize your process and map out your long-term goals. If you know what you're doing and where you're going, your tribe will come along for the journey.
- Trust in the process.

I conclude by reiterating that consistency and proper planning are the best ways to stay on top of your personal branding journey.

Free Chapter 7 Resources

I've designed a helpful guide to help you navigate this chapter's more in-depth and interactive secB tions. If you want to explore this in more detail, go to **dainwalker.com/resources/chpt7.** It's totally free, so make sure you don't miss out. You can also scan the QR code to get access.

Chapter 8

FIND COWS, COOK MEAT

As your content campfire grows, and your tribe grows, your campfire will develop into a village of dedicated fans (what I've been calling a *tribe*)—some of whom will actively seek ways to work with you beyond the means of your content.

It also won't necessarily take that long to reach this stage. I was able to monetize my offering—still creating potent content, but for others instead—by day 14. I've also taught my process to thousands of students, and many of my students were able to monetize their content starting from about day 60 to 90 (some even as early as their first week!). And many of them didn't have to overtly pitch or sell anything! They simply kept consistently producing quality daily content—and their tribe started to DM them asking for help.

Once you reach this stage—at the point of enquiry for your services—you'll want to have decided what niche you want to be known for: your x factor, your secret sauce, your thing. And then start creating a reputation for yourself. You want to become known for one thing in the same way that I initially became known as the "Instagram guy"—and then the "branding guy" once I discovered the niche I was best suited for. As stated in Chapter 5: Get Good Throwing Wood, it's okay if you pivot and keep working on your niche. You may be able to monetize your initial niche, but if you find that the inquiries don't align with what you want to sell, then you need to keep working on aligning your five key themes to attain the types of inquiries you're looking for.

Build Your Three Pillars

We're going to briefly revisit the trust hurdle approach from Chapter 7: Give Value, Earn Loyalty. There are three important components or pillars of what makes your personal brand a product and your campfire a valuable commodity. You want to clarify for yourself, and consistently and clearly broadcast to others, the answers to three questions:

- What makes you a **credible** figure of authority?
- What makes you **relevant** to your tribe?
- What makes you **reliable**?

The stronger these pillars are, the more valuable you will appear in your audience's eyes. The stronger these pillars are, the easier it will become for you to ask for money—and then, later, more money—from the opportunities that come your way. I can't overstate the sheer potency of nailing these for yourself. I believe these three pillars are the only reason I've achieved what I have.

Credibility

Your credibility tells your customers you're the greatest in the world at what your campfire/village is known for, your "one true thing." Credibility is (1) *what* you communicate to your tribe through your personal brand and (2) *why* you can solve their challenges. If you're lavishly giving them for free the content they need to solve their problem, why would they want to go to anyone else? This is why it's so essential to out-create the competition on content.

Credibility is, in part, in the size of your tribe. It's in the volume of your engagement. It's in how fervently your tribe becomes attached to you and your content. It's the testimonials you receive from happy customers. It's the raving reviews they leave on your Google page and website. It's the recognition you may get from a prestigious company or partnership.

No one can simply hand you credibility. It comes from relentlessly and consistently showing up. You must earn it by leading your tribe and serving your tribe better than any other tribe leader in your industry. You want your campfire to have the brightest flames, the tallest smoke plume, and the biggest group dancing around it—a fully immersed, engaged community.

Relevance

Relevance is the connection between what you offer and what your audience needs and seeks out. Creating relevance is all about building a safe haven where your tribe can hang out, a space where they can get warmth, get value, and get inspiration. Your social media campfire is that safe haven.

Think about how often and frequently you felt alone with your business challenges and obstacles. Relevance is the moment of connection, the moment of understanding when visitors realize they're no longer alone, that they don't feel so helpless, and that they're now part of a tribe that they share a like-mindedness with.

Your relevance is what makes you worth listening to, as in "This person understands me, understands my problem, and has the answers to help me." Your relevance is in how familiar you feel to your tribe. It's in your behavior, it's in how you see the world, and it's in how you think things should become.

Something I focus a lot of energy on with my tribe is being as relevant as possible to them by reminding them I'm human, that I feel and go through all the same things that they do. It's about ensuring that people don't feel alienated or like they're the only person going through the struggles of personal branding.

Reliability

It's crucial that as a personal brand you don't attempt to present yourself as better than someone or something else. It's about cultivating reliability. Personal branding isn't about being the best; personal branding is a game about being the unique version of yourself. It's a game of offering something that nobody else in the world is offering in a way that nobody else is offering it. Others also offer value; it's just not the value that *you* offer.

Differentiate Your Campfire

To be able to monetize your personal brand successfully, it must be distinctly clear what you offer. And so the first step in building a reputation is to clarify this for yourself. What do you want to be known for? And how does that desire lead to your product and service offering? And how can you ensure you're absolutely unambiguous?

I will show you how exactly to own an idea in the mind of your tribe so that they see you and your offering the way you want it to be seen. After all, building your personal brand is the art of cultivating a perception of who you are, why you exist, and how you can help them. To do this we want to find the one thing that will feed everything that your personal brand touches.

I think of this in terms of first money feeding second money and third money. My content and my website blatantly demonstrates that I specialize in branding. I teach brand education, brand strategy, and brand design for corporations and personal brands. I strive to be known for one thing: branding.

Now, beyond the many service offerings I have, there are other offerings that I don't mention to clients and I don't mention them in my content. They include, but are not limited to these offerings:

- Websites
- Shopify stores
- Marketing campaigns
- Advertising campaigns
- Advertising management
- User experience/user interface (UX/UI) for applications
- Product design
- Product photography
- Business consulting

Your objective is to rapidly place yourself in their mind as something new, something unique, something reliable. Do everything you can to differentiate yourself.

Now, if I tried to develop a reputation of expertise for all of these options, it would make my brand less potent and less effective (and less interesting) because it would blur what my specialty really is. But once a visitor becomes a tribe member and then a paying client, these services become unveiled and demystified. In other words, I maintain the approach of not trying to sell anything too overtly—even once the client decides to purchase.

Clients come to me to purchase branding services: what they want to be known for and how that is broadcast via social media. Now, if they're updating their branding—or branding a new company—they're going to need alignment (consistent messaging!) among all remaining parts of their brand: their websites, their marketing, their packaging, their UX/UI, their product photography, and everything else. But I don't initially mention all these services upfront, which we proudly offer, because I don't want my brand to be seen as "the one-stop shop," which can, in my opinion, dilute the weight of your core offering by casting too wide of a net. As mentioned in Chapter 6: Master the Smoke Signals, you don't want to be too clever. You want to be clear.

 Monetize Your Product

The biggest mistake I made with my early monetizing was that I offered anything and everything, which created too many things to juggle and a remarkable amount of pressure. It also introduced a lot of problems and chaos to my finances.

Because I had created too many product variables, I spent all my time putting fires out with clients; juggling everything became a total dumpster fire. I later learned to totally master one service until I got phenomenal results with it—then increase my pricing, then rinse and repeat. Only then did I start to trickle in additional service offerings. What this enabled me to do is streamline the money-making process. As each client went through the same process, I gained the experience of how long it took, and learned how to quickly and easily duplicate what I did with one client and apply it to another.

So, what was the one service I learned to totally master until I got phenomenal results? The first singular product suite that I sold was a content-creation package that I've outlined here.

Simple right? And if you think this looks expensive, you're right. The business owners I'd connected with were desperate. They knew they couldn't create their social media content themselves because they had

Package 1: $3,500 per month
- 10 social media posts a month

Package 2: $5,000 per month
- 20 social media posts a month

Package 3: $6,000 per month
- 30 social media posts a month

Add-on 1: +$500 per 10 posts
- Caption writing
- Hashtag research

Add-on 2: +$1,000 per 10 posts
- Post-optimization
- Post-scheduling

tried for years with their own employees and had failed. (This says nothing against the talent of those employees; they likely weren't given the authority to pitch a singular bold statement that didn't scream, "Buy me!") These business owners knew what effect they wanted, but they didn't know how to produce it. I convinced them I'd be able to produce exactly what they wanted. In fact, I was presenting such a solid case to these clients that I was selling these packages with all of the add-ons. Not only that, clients constantly asked what *else* I could do to help them.

The mess I'd previously made with selling everything got discarded. About the second month, I created a simple system: three options, two add-ons—that's all. (This remained the case for about two years.)

Again, I recommend that you first get yourself off the ground and monetize by doing one thing extremely well. Whatever you create for yourself, keep it simple, keep it duplicatable. And note: it doesn't have to be your forever product—it's what you'll initially have the means to handle *on your own* without needing to rely too much on others. Why? So you can always come through—solidifying your reputation with each client.

I like to call this initial offering your cash cow. A cash cow is not your forever product; it's your get-money-in-the-bank-right-now product. It's the product you get your business off the ground with, something that you can offer, sell, and fulfill with your eyes closed because it's something you're confident executing. In my case, I'd been learning the ropes of creating my own content for less than a month before I started selling these packages. By then, for me creating content was a cakewalk; for my clients it was a nightmare, so they were more than willing to outsource that to me.

Identify Candidates

So, what you want to do is find that first initial product that you can create an irrefutable offer for, create a system for, and sell. Monetization comes easily and frequently once you identify your golden cash cow. But how exactly do you do that? The tribe members who respond to what you're currently offering will likely identify it for you by telling you exactly what they want from you. And as previously stated in Chapter 6: Master the Smoke Signals, if they're asking for something you can't fulfill, you might need to consider changing your five key themes to accommodate for this.

So let's say you're focused on educating your tribe about a particular topic. You've positioned yourself as an expert on this topic, and you're con-stantly offering value for it. If your tribe grows around your campfire, and your content burns well, many members of your tribe will likely start ask-ing you questions that fall into a similar category, such as how to do some-thing in particular, or how to expand on what they've developed, thanks to you. They'll ask lots of questions; it's your job to identify the common denominator of those questions and figure out exactly what your cash cow should be.

What happened with me was my tribe repeatedly praised my work and asked if I could help them make content like mine. To which my reply was, "Sure!" Your tribe will tell you what they want to buy from you.

There are four main categories of what to look out for from your tribe to identify cash cow candidates. I'll flesh these out with examples from my own experience:

Identify What Their Problems Are
- My customers didn't know how to make content.
- My customers didn't have a brand to make content with.
- My customers didn't have a nice website to send the leads to.
- My customers wanted to pay me to solve their problems.

Identify Why They Need Their Problems Solved
- My customers wanted to update their digital branding.
- My customers wanted to create additional leads.
- My customers were tired of managing this work themselves.
- My customers could afford to outsource this work to an expert.

Create an Offer That Addresses Their Pain Points
- Using your five key themes, plot out what single service you could provide = your cash cow.
- Using your five key themes, create top-notch free content—derived from your planned offering—that presents solutions to your audience's problems.
- Continue to do this until tribe members ask you to help them with their problems.
- Get on a call with them and present your cash cow offering.
- Follow through with any leads.

Continue Adding Wood to Your Campfire
- Continue posting daily to stay top of mind.
- Find new angles to solve your tribe's problems.
- Continue giving away as much value as possible.

Exercise: Seek Out Your Cash Cow

For this exercise, I want you to start to ideate what product/service (cash cow) you can begin to offer to your tribe. To do this effectively, start with who your target audience is, then outline how you want them to perceive you. In my case, I originally wanted to be seen as a content creation specialist by small business owners. I then offered them the relief of creating and managing the content for them.

I identified early when producing content that this was a monetization opportunity. Your goal here is to do the same thing for yourself. Offer a service that's structured on your target audience and that solves a primary problem they have, and then deliver your content to create a perception in their mind that you're an expert at facilitating this solution for them.

Specify who your tribe members are:

> *For example: small business owners*

What do you want them to know you for?

> *For example: content creation specialist*

	List your tribe's top five problems.	What product could you create to solve this problem?	Describe exactly how the service will solve their problem.
	(e.g., struggling with content creation for their company)	*(e.g., sell content creation packages on a retainer)*	*(e.g., produce content and manage it for them, giving them time back)*
1			
2			
3			
4			
5			

Craft Your Cash Cow

Once you've identified which candidates you want to try to monetize, it's time to roll up your sleeves and put on a chef's hat. This is because I liken the process of developing a product or offering to a chef coming up with their own signature dish. Even if it's a staple like a burger, the ingredients they use might be different—or they might aim for unexpected flavor or unique presentation. Creating a signature dish takes lots of time experimenting with flavor profiles and cooking methods. And the most successful creations transform well-known dishes into something unexpected and highly memorable.

Your goal as a personal brand with a campfire is to become a chef of monetization. You're going to need to find your own style and your own method to create your own kitchen. Your goal—through experience, experimentation, and execution—is to learn how to cook something for your tribe that they can't purchase or experience anywhere else. Sure, other campfires sell burgers, but how do you craft a burger that's so unusual and so good that your reputation spreads to other campfires? You use the MEAT method.

 **MEAT**

M = Mold Your Product

No matter how much preparation you put into dreaming up your cash cow, it's impossible to picture in advance a detailed rendition of how it will turn out. So it's best to keep things organic initially. I call this process *molding*. In terms of the signature dish metaphor, the molding phase is when you're tinkering with your burger recipe and cooking method until you feel you have something worthy of putting on the fire. Take your time with this until you feel good about your initial offering.

E = Execute Your Product

This next phase is a bit entwined with the mold phase in the same way that different ingredients are mixed into the raw hamburger meat. Because we can't know how a product will flesh itself out, we need to be willing to go with the flow and begin to sell *something*—and take notes of all the details until we can figure it all out.

So, once you're ready to start offering to your tribe, it's time to execute. Make it known that you're dreaming up a signature recipe burger and that you're cooking it on your campfire. You'll get some initial takers, and they'll let you know what they think. In essence, the true molding of your product will result from the feedback your tribe gives you—"This burger is a bit too salty." "Maybe more umami?" "Is this quinoa?"—so let it happen naturally. Don't force it.

For each new customer in my execution phase, I worked to improve on my product and service offerings: slowly molding, slowly improving from one client to the next, slowly increasing my effectiveness in delivering a desired outcome. By just executing your best plan, you gain the most useful knowledge and insights on how to continue to improve.

A = Accelerate Your Production

Some find that their first product and service offering phase feels a bit slow and tedious. But masterpieces take time to develop, so you need to give yourself space to learn as you go. But, once you've established a product or service and it's working, your next objective is to accelerate: produce more, and more quickly. Oftentimes, to effectively accelerate production you'll need to also accelerate what you charge for it. Build up your momentum—and keep it up.

T = Transform Your Product

This phase could be experienced in one of two ways. If things are going great, then you continue the process of transforming your cash cow into something truly viable—based on the feedback you get, how well you implement the feedback that resonates for you, and how well you're able to perfect the entire process. If this applies to you with your first offering, hearty congratulations are in order.

The other and, statistically more likely, version is that you won't yet feel satisfied with your initial offering. It could be that it will simply take more time. It also could be that your offering is struggling—in which case you have to be willing to tweak it or even entirely transform it.

In my case, I was selling content creation for my first six months. But when I realized it was not exactly the offering I wanted to pursue, I pivoted. I shut down my content creation packages entirely and pivoted into workshopping and developing brand identity packages for my clients. I was willing to shift my business model entirely, which fortunately was the right thing to do.

If this happens for you as you grow your business—if an idea you loved loses its initial luster—hopefully the process of making money from something you're no longer enamored with will shine a spotlight on what you'd rather be doing instead. In my case, once I decided to shift away from content-creation packages, I simply started the MEAT process all over again with my next brand offering—working through the steps until I discovered exactly what I wanted to offer and precisely how I wanted to offer it.

It's through cycles of the MEAT process that you'll progressively identify what you want to be doing. Try to expand into the process; explore it without getting married to any one recipe, any one cooking method. Keep in close touch with your tribe, intently listening to their feedback. Allow yourself to organically transform and reconfigure, progressively moving toward finding that core offering that resonates the best with you.

My initial product suite no longer exists whatsoever in my current monetization offering. Yet, my initial year and set of services made me millions of dollars. A product I would now label as inferior, that I would label as amateur cooking, made me a lot of money and gave my clients a lot of value and nutrients. My point here is that you shouldn't get too tied down with the initial things that make you money. Nor should you deter yourself from selling services that you know you'll only sell in the short term to invest into growing your future service offerings. You should constantly seek to evolve and edit whatever you're cooking up over your campfire.

There are endless ways you can monetize your brand, just as there are endless meals you could cook over your campfire and offer to your tribe. When you completely apply yourself to the monetization process, you'll find your own way of creating products and services that you can concoct and deliver yourself. As a chef finds their own recipes through discovering different ingredients, you will find your own way of monetizing your personal brand.

Exercise: Levels of Language

This exercise derives from the relevance section from Chapter 7: Give Value, Earn Loyalty. To make your product or service relevant to the tribe, you need to fully understand what their needs are. Similarly, you must use communicative language about your product to ensure its merits are clear to everyone. Each of your tribe's members has their own sophistication level of the language *you* communicate with. So, for the language of your website and promotional materials, you'd phrase everything in what's called *plain writing* so that, to quote the United States' Plain Writing Act of 2010, your users can "Find what they need, understand what they find, and use what they find to meet their needs."[1]

But, as detailed in Chapter 7: Give Value, Earn Loyalty, it's also true that it's actually the one-on-one conversations that close the sale, so you'll need to tailor your phrasing to meet that of your tribe member—not in terms of their capacity to speak your language, but in terms of their comprehension of the product you offer. If they have a basic understanding of what you're offering, then you need to communicate it in a basic way. If they have an intermediate understanding of what you offer, then you'll want to communicate it in an intermediate way. If they have an expert understanding of what you're offering, then you must communicate it in an expert way.

Describe your cash cow in a basic way using plain language.

Next, phrase the same cash cow content in a more intermediate way for a member who understands the gist of what you offer but wants to learn more.

Now, rework your phrasing again to convey the same information but in an expert way for those who have a strong understanding of what you offer, and now want all the details.

Chapter Summary

In this chapter, I discuss the complexity and power of monetizing your personal brand. I use some personal examples, as well as those of my students, to show that you can accelerate your journey if you commit to doing it in 90 days:

Campfire to Village
* Although building a personal branding campfire is a long journey, it doesn't stop there. The next step—becoming a village that attracts more tribe members—is one that requires even more dedication.
* Consistent content creation over 90 days is the way to do this.
* If you approach your journey the right way, you can, like some of my students, start monetizing your product suite within 60 to 90 days.

Three Pillars of Personal Branding
* The three pillars are credibility, relevance, and reliability.
* Credibility is earned through consistency and via referrals and testimonials from your tribe.
* Relevance comes from always addressing your tribe's core needs.
* Reliability is about showing that you offer unique value.

Building a Reputation
* Deciding on a niche is crucial, but you can always pivot when you feel it's right to do so. You just need to always have one niche.
* Be clear, not clever, when starting out.

Monetization Strategies
* Master one service before expanding your offering.
* Create a cash cow that can serve you in the long run and feed back into your future product suites.

Identifying Your Cash Cow
* Observe audience feedback to identify common and recurring tribe needs and problems.

- Focus on identifying these problems, understanding why they need solutions, what offer will solve them, and how to continue adding value over time.

The MEAT Method
- You can explore your offering and audit it through what I call the MEAT method:
  - **M (Mold)**: Experiment and consistently refine your initial offering.
  - **E (Execute)**: Start selling your product and make sure to note down all levels of feedback from your tribe.
  - **A (Accelerate)**: Once your product is successful, begin increasing the production and output rate. You can even start increasing the price.
  - **T (Transform)**: Keep transforming your offering over time to ensure your tribe is satisfied. Don't be afraid to pivot.

Ultimately, this chapter's purpose is to show you the cyclical process of monetization when it comes to personal branding. Stay consistent and keep refining everything to make it work.

Free Chapter 8 Resources

I've designed a helpful guide to help you navigate this chapter's more in-depth and interactive secB tions. If you want to explore this in more detail, go to **dainwalker.com/resources/chpt8.** It's totally free, so make sure you don't miss out. You can also scan the QR code to get access.

SCAN ME

Chapter 9

COMMAND MOMENTUM, COLLECT MONEY

You'll probably spend a fair amount of time in this phase of the process. And it can be tough. So the first portion of this chapter offers reinforcement for how to weather the seasons of maintaining your business. And although some of you might be itching to venture toward greater heights, I do recommend you feel really solid with your cash cow before expanding your offerings. But when you're ready, the second portion of this chapter shows you exactly how to branch out into a wider realm.

 ## Maintain Your Momentum

There several crucial lessons to keep in mind as you develop within your monetization phase.

Understand Your Market

So, you've monetized your offering. You're making sales and you're making progress and fanning the flames. But it's important to keep a balanced view of where you go from here, and that calls for remembering your core, initial intention: creating quality content and sharing it with like-minded tribe members, whether or not an exchange of funds takes place. It's crucial to remember that your tribe comes for the warmth of your campfire, for the heat of your content. A few will be willing to buy, and will be hungry enough to do so, but they will be just a small percentage. But take heart: you can stoke additional hunger.

The plain truth is there will never be a time when 100% of your tribe is so engaged that they will all purchase your offering. In my experience, only 1% of that tribe will be willing to buy what you're cooking at any one time. But time doesn't stand still. The other 99% can smell the aroma of the meals you're cooking, and they can see the testimonials of the well-fed and satisfied 1%, and they will very much pay attention. Many will spread the word that you're an amazing cook—that you sell the best burgers in all the land—even though they've not yet purchased one themselves.

As surprising as it sounds, many of the 99% of the tribe who never buy from you promote your campfire to the 1% who will buy from you. I can't count the number of times I've sold a product to someone who was referred to me by someone who sat in my tribe for months—even years—without buying anything from me. But they told their friend or associate that I existed, promoted my campfire, and ultimately convinced others to purchase. In many cases, the 99% can be the reason the 1% will buy.

Perfect Your Pitch

Similarly, there's a talent to promoting what we offer in a manner that intrigues as many as possible while annoying as few as possible. We need to have a distinctly savvy sense of our tribe. We need to be mindful: we can't be too forceful or push something too prematurely. Pressure to fork over money will inevitably be a turnoff, and the tribe we spent so much time and energy and love trying to build will leave our campfire in search of a more simpatico campfire elsewhere.

However, we can't be too passive either—or no one will know we have a product or service to offer in the first place. So the goal is to make it known that you have something to offer readily available and suitable for their needs—that your burger is appetizing and exciting—but not to press the point too much.

This is because each of the members of the tribe will have a different appetite for what's on offer, and each will be at a different stage of their buying cycle. It's essential that you tailor your pitch to account for this discrepancy.

Take Stock and Stay Smart

When you start to monetize your personal brand effectively, it can be extremely tempting to ease up on your content creation because the money is flowing in handsomely. You can take a breather, right? Wrong. If you break your momentum, you sever the bonds that have been forged with the 99% who are marketing your offering. It's important to remember why the person who bought from you is there in the first place. They see the credibility and size of your tribe, they see the testimonials from others who have bought from you, and they found you only because the 99% promoted you for free. It's crucial you keep that fire burning hot, and it's important to keep the tribe 100% engaged—so that you can continue selling to the very few hungry enough to actually buy.

Grow Organically

As your tribe grows around your campfire, it's your role and responsibility as the village leader to know how to adapt and offer products and services your tribe wants—and, more important, to deliver them effectively. At the same time, it's important to keep in mind that not all tribe members want the same solutions so there is no way to expand your offerings to satisfy your entire tribe.

You must allow your product and service creation to organically reveal itself. As you offer variations or innovations to your tribe, make note of their reactions. Allow your tribe to form your product suite. Allow their feedback to guide you. Every industry has different problems and different types of tribes. Make use of those differences.

 # Expand Your Offerings

Your cash cow is your bedrock product. In time, once you've established some contractors or employees who can help you fulfill deliverables, you can start to leverage your cash cow to sell other products and services when you're ready to expand.

Like I said: those three content packages with two add-ons were the foundational product that got me established—that got me effectively monetized. When I later started selling additional services, it wasn't because I'd decided to expand my offerings; it was because my clients requested them:

- Can you update my brand strategy?
- Can you help me with my logo?
- Can you help me select my colors + fonts?

- Can you build me a website to send my customers to?
- Can you help me set up some ads?
- Can you train my team to do this for me?

To all of these questions, my answer to my clients was "Hell, yes!" That is, once I had enough money coming in, and a fully functioning system, I started to hire contractors to take over the deliverables. That freed me up to talk to clients and sell more packages. Only then was I in a position to start offering what I call *second money*.

As you might imagine from the name, second money doesn't derive from what the customer initially came for you to help with; it results from the additional issues your solution reveals—and what clients later request help with. In my case, solving my clients' initial objective—content creation, not just completing it but completing it well—revealed additional angles of branding that merited attention. For example, perhaps they didn't have a logo, or they hadn't identified colors or fonts they liked. Very often they needed to update their website to receive and effectively make use of all the new traffic that would be coming in.

So I didn't have to offer or promote the second-money offerings as part of what my personal brand was known for; I just needed to be known for my cash cow. Back then, my cash cow was content creation; today, it's branding. To this day I only need to be known for branding; as mentioned in Chapter 8: Find Cows, Cook Meat, I still don't promote everything we do at Rivyl.

This is how you identify your niche while simultaneously getting everything you want. You keep your offering simple, clear, concise, and easy to understand. You make your campfire about your big cash cow, telling the whole world your genius is that one core thing. With the additional issues revealed from completing the cash cow deliverable, you ramp up to ensure you can fulfill whatever second money deliverables are requested.

At the end of my first year (yes, I know, this is outside the 90 days; however, I hope this gives you something to aspire to), my secondary offerings included the following:

- Logo design: $2,500
- Color psychology + fonts: $2,000

- Content strategy workshop: $5,000
- Content strategy guideline: $5,000
- Website creation: $10,000–$15,000
- Ad creation: $500 per graphic
- Ad management: $2,500 per month

In time, I was often able to upsell these second products on the first sales call because the client realized that, in order to get the absolute most out of their content creation, they'd benefit from having all these assets working in tandem (and it's easier doing that with the same vendor).

So your goal is to do something similar for yourself. For that, see the next sidebar.

Phase 1
- Identify your cash cow.
- Become known for your cash cow (and that only).
- Sell your cash cow.
- Create systems and infrastructure around yourself so you can rinse and repeat.

Phase 2
- Listen to your clients to identify the additional issues your cash cow reveals.
- Create systems and infrastructure around yourself so you can expand to include second money offerings.
- Add the second money offerings to your cash cow selling efforts. Rinse and repeat.
- Focus on selling, hiring others to handle fulfilment as much as possible.

This process takes time, and thus requires a lot of patience. It will take a serious commitment to cooking various offerings at your campfire. In my case, years. Some of these you'll burn beyond edibility. Some will look appetizing but taste terrible. But this is to be expected. All you can do is maintain goodwill with your tribe, learn from mistakes, and steadily improve your cooking skills.

As years go by, your ability to produce content will improve, your ability to grow a tribe will improve—as will your ability to cook up amazing services and products.

Pitch Your Village

Up through the process of perfecting your cash cow—meaning you're posting content, closing sales, and fulfilling those sales—you're essentially still a campfire, albeit a large one. But once the time comes to expand your offerings, you essentially develop into a village. When that happens, you want to expand from considering how your tribe sees you to considering how companies see you.

As you grow in fame with your personal brand, companies will begin to look at you as a product they can leverage for their own needs. Fortunately, you can leverage their offers for your own needs. For example, big event companies pay known speakers to present at their conferences. The event company wants one thing: bums on seats. In turn the speaker wants two things: payment for their time and keynote, and increased fame. So, let's say you accept a speaking engagement. The event company wins; they get ticket sales. You as a speaker win payment and exposure to a new potential tribe. The audience wins because they get to enjoy all the content from the event.

But it's important that you realize that what's truly happening here is you as a speaker would be used like a commodity, like a product. It might feel unnatural to talk about yourself in this way, and it might even conjure up a sense of imposter syndrome. I had to become comfortable placing a price tag on my value. I had to become comfortable placing a price tag on my brand equity, on my content's ability to draw an audience, and so on.

Sometimes I still feel odd looking at myself as a product. But in order to grow, you'll need to develop this skill as well, because it's how businesses will begin to see you.

Price Your Pitch

So, how exactly do you justify putting a price tag on yourself? You don't! At least, you don't need to *justify* anything. You just decide what your time is worth, and you ask for it, plain and simple.

There's no secret recipe to pricing yourself. It's just a matter of understanding that you are a product that's for sale—and what price you put on yourself is up to you. My only advice is not to shortchange yourself; simply ask yourself, "What would be desirable compensation for the time and effort it would take for me to fulfill this engagement?" This amounts to the time you'd spend preparing your talk, the time you'd spend traveling there and back, and the time you'd not be spending tending to your business as a result. Factor in the benefit you'd glean from the increased exposure. Once you've determined a sum that works for you, ask for it.

When starting out, I often received enquiries to speak. (I gave my first talk at about month three.) I initially did it for free because I was purely happy to gain the experience of speaking in front of live audiences. After I had spoken a few times and felt comfortable with my ability to maintain a stage presence and speak to an audience, I started to ask for a fee: initially $500, then $3,000, then $5,000, then $10,000, then $25,000, then $50,000+.

As it happens, an additional great benefit I have as a speaker who owns a branding agency is the opportunity to do keynotes to rooms of high-caliber business owners. Because of my keynote and branding expertise, I've produced over $1,000,000 in revenue for my agency. So, sometimes you get paid directly; other times, you can leverage the opportunity and pay yourself indirectly, as I do for my agency. Whatever the outcome, you just need to be happy with it—and so long as you're happy, keep doing it. For me, speaking was never about the money; I genuinely enjoy sharing my content with live audiences. It is always nice, however, to get paid to do something you love so much.

So how do you decide how to price yourself? Start by identifying the number of followers you currently have, then ask yourself the following questions:

OTHER THAN THE DIRECT EXCHANGE, WHAT ELSE WOULD YOU GET?

Would you get the opportunity to interact with a new audience? Would you get free exposure on their platforms? Don't look at just the immediate effect—look at the entire picture.

WHAT WOULD YOU BE HAPPY TO BE PAID?

Be as audacious as you like; decide what number makes you happy and put it out there. You will be shocked at who will say yes! I can't count how many times I proposed a higher price than I was comfortable saying just to have it be immediately accepted.

HOW WOULD YOU BE PAID?

There are many forms of payment. For example, when I speak about my company in front of an audience, I generate many potential clients. Our account director converts these enquiries into paying customers, so in this example I'd be getting paid in **exposure**. Another one is **access**; more than once exchanging my service (my talk) for just getting the opportunity to network has been a game changer. However you slice it, people see your personal brand as valuable. The bigger you get, the more money you can ask for, and the more you can barter in exchange.

All this talk of high-flying speaks, of course, to when your village is expanding into an empire. More on that in the next chapter.

Exercise: Product or Service Price Progression

It's important when learning to price your products and services that you acknowledge you have a starting point that you're initially going to be paid. However, ensure you don't get stuck there. I see too many people progress their payment and price structure far too slowly. I recommend you scale your pricing as fast as possible.

For example, in my first month I was willing to be paid $50 for a logo, then $250, then $500, $5,000, and so on. Give yourself permission to charge as much as you like.

I want you to list and price all the products or services you have a desire to sell. For this exercise, I suggest use the products you identified in the exercise in Chapter 8: Find Cows, Cook Meat. Then set a price that you're willing to be initially paid, then a desired price you wish to work toward. It's important to keep in mind the how and what are the actionable steps you will need to take to bridge the gap between these two price points.

The idea here is that you progress and increase your price as your brand grows as you increase your experience and your personal brand. For example, you might price your first logo design for $50; however, ideally you might want to charge $10,000 per logo design. To bridge the gap between these price points, you might need to increase your portfolio.

What is the product?
-
-
-
-
-

Where am I willing to start?
-
-
-
-
-

Where do I want to be?
-
-
-
-
-

What will bridge the gap?
-
-
-
-
-

Chapter Summary

In this chapter, I emphasize the importance of maintaining momentum in all aspects of your personal brand. This can be achieved by focusing on a few key things:

Build Momentum
- Don't expand too early. Build a steady momentum before adding things to your product suite. Stick with your cash cow until you're ready.

Understand Your Market
- Focus on creating quality content that serves to reward the loyalty of your tribe, even those who aren't paying customers.
- In my experience, only roughly 1% of tribe members are true and consistent paying customers. The other 99% usually take it on themselves to market you instead. This is invaluable.

Perfect Your Pitch
- You need to tailor your sales approach to your specific tribe and niche. Don't be forceful. Be genuine and offer true value.
- Your tribe isn't just one entity. It is made up of different people with different levels of purchasing power. Always keep that in mind.

Stay Calm, Dedicated, and Calculated
- Keep targeting both the 1% and the 99% at all times.

Grow Organically
- Adapt your products to the genuine needs of your tribe.
- Focus on value and not greed, and organic growth will follow.

Know When to Expand
- Once you've fine-tuned your cash cow and are ready to expand, do so without fear. Back yourself.
- Make sure you respond to clients to develop what I call *second money*—a way to diversify and expand your existing offerings.

Become a Village

* Once you've established your product suite, know your tribe, and have experienced high levels of success, you can start transitioning into a village.
* Becoming a village means you will be seen in more favorable lights by other villages.

Become a Product

* Don't be afraid to see yourself as a product or commodity; people will already do this.
* Sell yourself genuinely by focusing on the value you provide.

This chapter is essentially a comprehensive guide for navigating the different phases of personal branding maintenance and expansion.

Free Chapter 9 Resources

I've designed a helpful guide to help you navigate this chapter's more in-depth and interactive secB tions. If you want to explore this in more detail, go to **dainwalker.com/resources/chpt9.** It's totally free, so make sure you don't miss out. You can also scan the QR code to get access.

Chapter 10

BLUEPRINT YOUR FUTURE EMPIRE

The entirety of my approach to monetizing personal brands is encapsulated in what I've termed the *empire blueprint*. This framework will serve any kind of personal brand, whether in entertainment, education, or anything else. The objective of this blueprint is for you to eventually model your product or service suite on a map of your empire, from entry-level items to high-ticket items and everything in between.

To be seen as an empire builder of personal branding is to be seen as having the ability to offer something to everyone at all price levels and at all stages of purchasing. The greater your ability to connect a product and service offering to the masses, the greater brand power you will create for yourself, the more leverage and trust you can cultivate with your tribe to create unlimited potential to monetize whatever offer you desire.

Identify Your Tribe's Means

The more people your products can positively affect, the happier your tribe will become—and, like loyal and devoted fans, if they buy an affordable product and love it, then they're likely to hop right into the next product offering. The idea is if someone's looking to jump straight into the high-ticket and high-value products, they can, but if they're not ready to go all in, there's also something for them to eat at more accessible levels. It's up to you to make sure that your personal brand is available for all members of your tribe, and you want it to be known that you have brackets of entry.

If you're in the position to roll out the entire blueprint all at once, by all means, go ahead. However, if you're not yet capable of executing the entire blueprint, that's okay—you just want to start somewhere. So if you're starting with just one, start with what I call the *main course*. But to develop an effective main course offering, it certainly helps to understand how and where you would focus your energy on expanding your products. That way, as you expand your offerings, you're not reengineering your original offering in its entirety; rather, you're adding it on as an additional or alternative offering.

Your empire blueprint will begin small and then scale to fill every gap in the market that a personal brand can. Ultimately, you'll want your brand to have as much market penetration and cut-through as possible.

Think about it this way: as a tribe member steps up to your campfire to take a close look at your offerings, you want something available for them at a level that makes sense to them. That's because they might be hungry enough to buy everything you have to offer—but not (yet) have the purchasing power to match.

These are the concerns you want to be mindful of:

Your tribe's appetite level: Ask yourself these important questions about what your tribe thinks while surveying your offerings. Do they want them? Do they feel they need them? Do they have a desire to begin working with you? By carefully engineering your content to give maximum value that solves the problems your tribe is having every day, you'll be able to increase their appetite for your offering. If you rarely post content or your content is irrelevant to their needs, their appetite will decrease. The content on your campfire will increase or decrease the appetite of your tribe depending on how you post, what you post about, and how frequently your posts are helpful. By ensuring that you're top of mind every day—and from getting feedback from your followers—you'll be able to maximize the appetite of your tribe.

Your tribe's trust level: Increasing their appetite for solving their problem is one thing; earning their trust is another. As covered in Chapter 7: Give Value, Earn Loyalty, you want to focus on building trust with your tribe—early and often. Think of this as a form of currency. The greater trust you earn with your tribe, the greater the conversion on your product and service offering. What tilts a tribe member into the buying cycle is when their appetite meets trust.

Your tribe's currency level: This one concerns members' means to engage with your offering—what resources they have available to them. The most obvious aspect of their purchase power is whether they can readily afford you—or find the means to afford you. The higher their appetite and the more they trust you, the more they'll be willing to pay. But there is another, equally important aspect to currency level. As for the tribe members who have trust and appetite but not the means to pay you (yet)—have trust in them. These tribe members will likely advocate for you and promote your page for free; they may even set a goal to eventually purchase from you. Depending on where they live, what they do for work, and even the time of the year, their purchasing power will fluctuate. But as long as you remain top of mind, there's a chance they'll want to engage in some way.

Your tribe might offer these important offerings:

- Their time (comments, questions, DMs, etc.)
- Their details (email, phone, location, etc.)
- Their network (referrals)
- Their promotion (sharing you with their audience)

I recommend that you not look at your tribe from the perspective of monetization alone. View them from this wider perspective. Members of your tribe who don't pay you directly can pay you indirectly by boosting the reach of your content and personal brand to others who don't yet know you exist. What grows income for your brand is day-trading attention, time, effort, trust, and networking to create more opportunities and a greater relationship with your tribe around your campfire.

Prepare Your Empire's Menu

The best way to draft your empire's menu is to think of the customer journey and your offerings as a chef's menu. The way I break this concept down is in the figure that follows.

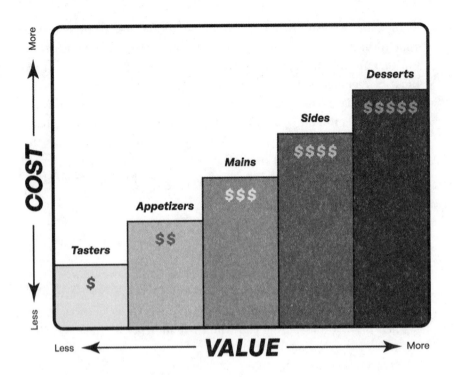

Taste Tester (Freemium)

To bridge the gap and increase your tribe's appetite, you need to start with taste testers. This is a product beyond your free social media offering to pull your tribe closer to committing to your product suite. It's a way to earn trust, generate leads, collect email addresses, and build your database.

The following are the typical product:

- Ebooks
- Free webinars
- Free courses
- Free community chat groups
- Free live calls
- Free events
- Podcasts

- Exclusive newsletters
- Long-format video content
- Downloadable exercises
- Downloadable worksheets
- Downloadable checklists
- Downloadable audits
- Downloadable resources
- Downloadable kits
- Downloadable templates
- Downloadable keynotes

Essentially, taste testers are resources that you're willing to give away in order to generate more appetite for your brand.

If someone in your tribe is enjoying your content and believes what you offer *could* solve their pain points, then they will grow a closer relationship with your brand. If the tribe member experiences a portion of your process and realizes that what you offer *does* solve their pain points, then you're essentially warming them up to become a lead for your other product offerings. And to keep your leads warm, you can contact your tribe for additional freemium items and additional taste-testers.

You may fear that giving free taste testers away might dilute your core offering. But this isn't the end of the journey. The taste tester is to convince the buyer of your inherent value. If they feel the value exchange for the time they invested in your taste tester is so good they should have paid for it, then you've earned their trust, their appetite, and their purchase power.

Appetizer (Hooks)

Appetizers are essentially the same formats as your freemium taste testers—they're just paid for. Think about appetizers like low-hanging fruit: your offerings that are so affordable that they're essentially a no-brainer for your tribe to invest in, assuming you have their trust.

Appetizers include the following:

- Physical books
- Audio books

- Workbooks
- Journals
- Exercises
- Paid webinars
- Paid courses
- Paid community groups
- Paid bootcamps
- Paid events
- Paid speaking engagements
- And so on

The core function of your appetizers is to give enough value to your tribe that they level up their relationship with you. Essentially, the low-hanging-fruit products and services convince them to purchase—to cross over from follower to customer, establishing a commercial relationship in exchange for curated high value.

In my case, my taste tester products solve just enough of one of the tribe's problems for them to realize they need more to comprehensively solve all their problems. But the appetizer product should in and of itself actually solve a problem (whether big or small). In other words, it's not just one cog in a machine—for which they'd need to buy all the other parts in order to have something worth having. In my case, an appetizer could be seen as this book you're reading. I decided to put all the value I possibly could within the confines of the limited pages of this book. In the event you find this book valuable, and it increases your appetite, you just might consider moving up my empire blueprint to buy something more comprehensive. That's the whole point of an appetizer—to leave you satisfied yet hungry for more.

Appetizers are products with a large reach that you can distribute through channels that enable you to grow and connect with strangers who could become paying members of your tribe.

This way, if a tribe member consumes your appetizer and then realizes you'd solve their problem much easier or better than they could do themselves, this increased appetite and realization will likely inspire them to purchase products higher in your product offering suite.

 ## Main Course (Primary Moneymaker)

Your main course is your *primary* offering. If you've accurately identified the primary problems your tribe is looking to solve, then it's likely you've found your main course. Here are some examples of main course products:

- One-on-one coaching
- Group consultations
- Small- to medium-sized subscription community groups
- In-depth online courses
- Paid speaking engagements
- Paid bootcamps
- Paid workshops
- Paid strategy
- Paid services
- Paid products
- And so on

My main course items when I started my personal brand were as follows:

- Content creation services
- Content strategy
- Logo design
- 1:1 consulting and coaching services
- Graphic design services

Your main course is your main moneymaker. It's where you'll want to invest 80% of your time because to make serious money as a personal brand requires serious attention to detail, and because your main course is the offering you want your personal brand to be known for. For me, because I wanted to be known for branding, I evolved my main course away from content creation and into brand creation. You might also find that the first main course products you cook up will evolve, change, and evolve again.

You'll want your main course to be hands-on, offering your tribe access to you. The more credible you become, the greater your tribe will grow—and the greater will be their desire and appetite to work with your brand.

Your main course must be something that you are confident you can handle and deliver. If you can't nail it personally, upskill yourself to effectively manage bringing in talented contractors who can deliver exactly what your client needs. Your goal with your initial clients is to go far above and beyond their expectations. This way you can create case studies and collect testimonials to demonstrate your value to others.

Side Dishes (Add-Ons + Upsells)

Your side dishes are what I referred to in Chapter 9: Command Momentum, Collect Money as second money products. Side dish products are additions, upsells, and extras—extensions to your main course.

For many tribe members who've decided to work with you, an add-on becomes an easy decision. It's like when you're at the checkout of a supermarket, you throw some extra items in your cart. Or when you're at a fast food chain, for a few extra bucks you can have add-ons to your meal. For example, let's say you have a content creation client who asks, "Can you also write my captions and post the content for me?" That extra $1,500 a month on top of the initial $3,500 per month content package is the equivalent of their getting fries with their burger.

Another great thing about side dish products is you can use them as a deal closer in the event the client is on the fence about your main course product, because they'll see that you offer even more value.

When presented with the opportunity to sell something to solve a client's main problem, you want to take the opportunity to solve additional problems that stem from their main problem. In other words, if your main course will solve their main problem, your side dishes will solve their side problems.

These are some of the side dishes I offered to my content creation clients in the past:

- Researching optimal post times
- Posting content at those optimal times
- Writing the caption that's paired with each piece of content

- Researching the hashtag groups they should use to maximize their reach
- Writing the hashtags that are paired with each piece of content
- Running monthly reports and audits to know how we can improve their growth and effectiveness of their content
- Ideation sessions so I can collaborate monthly with them on what to post about in the first place
- Supporting the client with their engagement; if people DM them or comment on their posts I would help manage this engagement on their behalf
- Writing their bio descriptors for their profiles
- Editing a nice photo of their face for their profile picture
- Updating their banners, their links, and their product descriptors

In almost every case, a client reached out to *me* to make their content. At appropriate junctures during the consultation meetings and proposal calls, once I had a greater sense of their situation, I'd reveal that there were additional aspects to their content creation that they needed to think about.

You'll want to do the same with your side dish products. List out all the additional items that would enable the client to get the most impact out of your main course offering. Anyone who sees this list will get, in turn, a much stronger sense of your expertise.

This is why you want to begin with your main course and reverse-engineer all the side dishes: to maximize your impact. In many ways, your taste testers and appetizers should reveal the complexity of solving their problem. This might make them realize that attempting to solve their problem themselves could end up being the wrong decision: taking longer, costing more, and producing a lower-quality solution than if they pay you to do it—either with them or for them.

Now, your "do it for them" products, in my opinion, should be your most expensive product offerings in your empire blueprint. This is because the tribe members seeking these deluxe services have the resources to use their purchasing power to save time and energy. The greater their purchasing power, the more likely they'll want you to do more of the work. That's why you want your empire blueprint to span so wide. The more explicit you delineate all that can be done—and needs to be done, for some clients—the better they comprehend just how comprehensive your entire package is and why you charge what you charge.

Dessert (Top-Tier)

Your dessert offerings are the cherry on top of everything else. In my case, about 15% of my clients were willing to go all in, paying the big bucks to have me completely solve all their problems. These are the hardcore tribe members, and they have extremely high purchasing power.

For example, when I was still focusing on content creation, my dessert items included the following:

* Brand identity design guide
* Photography guide
* Package design
* Website development
* Product development
* Service development

Dessert products are more than side dishes; they're lateral products that solve other problems that your main course offering doesn't include. The reason I label these dessert products and not additional main courses is because, based on the way I heavily pitched my main courses only, clients didn't come to me to solve these problems, generally speaking.

When you begin to expand your main course offering into dessert territory, you're expanding your product categories into something you may not even be aware of immediately. For example, in my first year, I sold hundreds of thousands of dollars' worth of websites to my clients—clients who'd come to me to get content creation only. About 15% of them ultimately opted for the full banquet of my products. My dessert products were things I hired others to fulfill—first contractors, and eventually employees.

You want to capitalize on these scenarios with product offerings that solve every possible problem your client has. And yet, I also suggest you hold off developing your dessert options until you've mastered selling your main course and side dishes. But even before you're ready, you'll want to identify these hardcore tribe members as soon as possible. You can do this by carefully diagnosing all of their problems on your initial consultation calls. In the event where you identify additional problems, simply ask the client if they'd like some assistance with that. In the event they say no, it doesn't mean you'll never get the chance again. Once the client appears to be satisfied with their main course, this is an ideal time to say to them, "Hey, would you like dessert with that?" Similar to being in a restaurant, in some cases, they'll say yes. It's important not to let a possible opportunity like this slip by.

To SUM UP, ONCE YOU PUT IN ALL THE EFFORT TO GROW A TRIBE, warm them up with content, offer them free taste testers, sell them appetizers—and then main courses and side dishes—introduce an expanded product suite—your dessert—to solve their additional problems and leave them completely sated and satisfied.

 ## Blueprint Your Empire

You can't build your empire blueprint all at once. But, as I said, if you loosely framework what your entire suite of products will become, it becomes easier to decide when and where you will focus your resources. Just keep in mind that all your product suites must orbit your main course. Everything else is either a lead-in or a supplement to your main course. If you design and promote these offerings effectively, your tribe, your customers, and your market will develop a complete understanding of you and your personal brand.

Fast-forward to today. My current empire blueprint is as follows:

Taste testers: Podcast, long format content, webinars, free events, downloadable workbooks/checklists, email newsletter, and so on

Appetizers: My books, online courses, paid events, paid boot camps, paid consulting, and so on

Main course: My branding agency Rivyl, which offers strategy, design, workshops, identity, keynote speaking, and so on

Side dishes: Logo design, brand naming, photography guides, photo shoots, product design, package design, and so on

Desserts: Website design and development, UX/UI design, app design and development, client course creation, marketing, advertising, content creation, brand activation, e-commerce services, and so on

Building my empire blueprint has been five years in the making. But the work is never finished. My team at Rivyl and I are constantly tinkering with it: crafting, editing, and updating all of my product suite, always looking for holes and listening to client feedback on how we can improve everything, front to back.

I say this to impress on you what's possible when you simply start with the stuff you can control. Start with the things you're great at and build from there. Again, most can't create a monetization empire within a short time frame—I doubt that would even be an effective approach. But it does help to know what it takes to build a monetization empire: an ever-evolving empire blueprint plan. If you don't know how to fill all the levels yet, that's fine; focus on the main course. But if you can at the very least ideate what your empire blueprint could potentially become, you'll dramatically increase the likelihood of one day building your own empire using personal branding in the way I have.

Exercise: Your Future Empire Blueprint

Make a list of your future empire blueprint. My suggestion here is that you include everything and anything that you would consider possibly selling. Not that you would activate all of these now; rather, it's good to know what services you're going to begin with and what services you plan to unlock later. Having this comprehensive list will help you ensure that your eventual empire blueprint lines up with everything in your product suite.

Once you've completed your list, if you'd like to take this further, highlight the ones you're going to monetize first. Then focus, as I suggested, on your main course products first and reverse-engineer your product suite from there. As mentioned in Chapter 6: Master the Smoke Signals, get the feedback of the inquiries from your five key themes to ensure you're addressing all of your tribe's core problems with your content. In the event that your themes and main course products don't align, you need to go back and make sure your five key themes are in sync with your tribe's true problems. This way, you will effectively monetize your main course offering.

Taste Testers	Appetizers	Mains	Side Dishes	Desserts
• • • • •	• • • • •	• • • • •	• • • • •	• • • • •
• • • • •	• • • • •	• • • • •	• • • • •	• • • • •

Chapter Summary

In this chapter, I introduce the empire blueprint, a comprehensive framework for personal brand monetization and acceleration. No matter what industry you're in, the empire blueprint helps you develop key strategies for product suite construction, tribe understanding, and trust building.

I find it easier to break down your product suite into a chef's menu, with you as the head chef.

- **Taste testers (freemium):** These are free resources of value that you can offer, such as ebooks, webinars, podcasts, and more. They help drive engagement and build trust.
- **Appetizers (hook):** These are your first paid offerings that prime tribe members to come back and purchase more things from you, such as books, courses, and events. These help convert your tribe members into paying customers and leave them wanting more.
- **Main courses (primary moneymakers):** This is your core offering, representing the primary products or services that you focus on— your cash cow—such as consulting and coaching. This is where the majority of your paying tribe members will gravitate toward, so this should be your focus.
- **Side dishes (add-ons and upsells):** These are additional products and services that can enhance your main course offerings, such as photography guides or even brand design guides.
- **Desserts (top-tier):** These are your high-end offerings that only a select few people will go for. This is best suited for tribe members with high purchasing power.

The point of this chapter is to make sure that you have an easily understandable framework that you can keep coming back to, helping you develop and maintain consistency with your product suite.

Free Chapter 10 Resources

I've designed a helpful guide to help you navigate this chapter's more in-depth and interactive secB tions. If you want to explore this in more detail, go to **dainwalker.com/resources/chpt10.** It's totally free, so make sure you don't miss out. You can also scan the QR code to get access.

Chapter 11

IMPORT AND EXPORT YOURSELF

et's say that, during your 90-day brand plan, your campfire burned bright with content logs and you built impressive momentum. Once you establish a small selection of products and have successfully monetized your personal brand . . . what next?

Well, your campfire does not exist on its own; it exists in a marketplace and a world full of campfires—literally millions of content creators with their very own tribes, campfires, villages, and empires. Given this reality, as a successful tribe leader of your very own empire-to-be, how can you leverage the beginnings of your success in partnership and cohort with others doing the same for themselves? It's at this stage that you'll want to do more than just the dogged work of consistency and momentum. You'll want to capitalize on your success as an entrepreneur by upping your game in terms of self-promotion.

If you work to position yourself as a leading authority on your topic and a master of unique solutions for problems in your industry, and if you establish strong relevance and memorability, then you have a lot to barter with. Your tribe can become a mechanism by which you can trade with companies and other campfires in exchange for opportunities, partnerships, and additional monetization avenues.

You see, once others catch wind of your following, your roaring campfire, and your ability to monetize yourself, you become a beacon in the wilderness that can attract others who'd be interested in consulting and conducting business with you. In my case, the greater my personal tribe grew, the greater my bartering chips became: for new opportunities for me, my companies, and ultimately even my tribe. This call can be a mutually beneficial arrangement—after all, the more you fine-tune your offering, the more you provide to your tribe, so you'll want to keep an eye out for such opportunities.

Access Roads

This final chapter in our journey together discusses how you can best leverage all that you've built to create even greater opportunities: via what I call *access roads*. Your campfire paired with your 90-day brand plan is your momentum builder, and your products are your monetizers. Access roads are your amplifiers (remember how we discussed amplifiers in Chapter 3: Slay the Time Vampires?); they're how you add weight to your brand and validate your success—to then be exported and imported in cohort with other brands and campfires.

Think of access roads as routes between your campfire and other campfires—campfires with substantial tribes whose members might be very interested in what you offer. But access roads don't just expand your fame and fan base; the result isn't your campfire plus another campfire. The result is your campfire *times* another campfire. Looking at it another way, if your reach is, let's say, to 100 people, and another campfire is also 100, the result wouldn't be 200. It would be 1000+, because your reach multiplies through their tribe members and networks—it doesn't just add together without any additional benefit. The benefits and opportunities expand exponentially.

To follow are just a few of the many opportunities access roads can facilitate. The first set concerns the most obvious benefit of access roads: mutual trade. The following are all goods you can import and export along your access roads.

Sponsorships

The bigger your tribe, the more potent your campfire, the more likely companies might reach out to you to have you feature their products or services in the form of a sponsorship. Some sponsorships involve monetary income, either as a one-time deal or to retainers where the paychecks are ongoing; others are worth leveraging purely to add status and credibility to your personal brand. These can be thought of as mutually beneficial sponsorships that serve to market both parties. For example, I've received products to be featured and highlighted on my podcast and on my content feed—chocolate bars from MrBeast's Feastables and the hydration and energy drink brand Prime, care of its two founders, influencer and wrestler Logan Paul and influencer and boxer KSI. (Both products were launched in January 2022.) Both companies' marketing teams decided my campfire was worthy of creating an access road to, and so they approached me, hoping to facilitate mutually beneficial free marketing. The weight and credibility of these trending brands inspired us to produce content with their products, which in turn opened up direct communication with other global brands.

But it did even more than that. It also sent a signal—more of a shock-wave, actually—through my community. That such global brands were interested in working with us communicated that we'd reached a new level of credibility and status—which meant that this one access road opened up the opportunities for additional access roads with more potential sponsors wanting to collaborate with us.

This is all thanks to the fact that people love to follow success. Crowds draw crowds.

So, how could this happen for you? Sponsorships can come to anyone with an identifiable tribe that others want to market to. Every tribe typically shares similar needs and shares similar demographics. That means that your tribe, in most cases, will represent a collective belief, a collection of like-minded people who see the world similarly and have similar purchasing habits. Sponsors know this, and so they want to put their brand front and center in your campfire, paying you to endorse their goods to your tribe in hopes of putting eyeballs on their products or services. It's about making an investment in your personal brand.

If you receive a sponsorship offer in which they're willing to pay you, try to make the sponsorship content as genuine as possible to fit in alongside your standard content. When we showcase sponsors, we don't blatantly promote or advertise or attempt to activate our audience to buy. We simply showcase the sponsored brand along with what we were already doing with our content. If our tribe decides to engage and buy . . . great; if not, that's fine, too. We get paid anyway, and we know we honored the original agreement. Keeping the integrity of your personal brand and your partnerships is integral here. After all, the more successful your ability to march your tribe down the access road between you and your sponsor, the more likely they are to return and continue to conduct business with you.

However, if the sponsor isn't willing to pay you but their brand has a strong standing in the marketplace, you can leverage showcasing their brand in order to open up a stronger partnership. You can even validate your worth as a personal brand publicly by highlighting that you're sought after for business opportunities, which signals to your tribe credibility, status, and value. If you accept this sort of agreement, watch to see how beneficial the sponsorship turned out to be. This will help you decide how to respond about the next sponsorship you're offered.

Partnerships

Partnerships are any business relationships you develop with companies and personal brands. As such, they're access roads between you and entities who offer services that you don't. For example, we refer all of our clients who need legal support and trademarking for their branding to our business partners who offer those services—in other words, we export our clients down an established access road so they can purchase solutions that we don't offer. In return, we might receive free services or a referral fee kickback as thanks for sending them easy business. It's about ensuring that everyone benefits. This is the best way to create, foster, and maintain relationships that will bolster the effectiveness and growth of your brand.

From my experience, the best partnership access roads exist at the fringes of my territory—such as in the example just described: when I can no longer serve a client, but I have a partner who can take the client's hand and take care of them from there. We do this with advertisement firms on completing our clients' branding, with trademarking firms on completions of logo marks, and even with product manufacturing companies on completion of package design. There's no end to the potential relationships you can build this way.

The best part is that everyone wins. Your clients benefit because they were handed a reputable expert for a problem they needed solved, and they will thank you for it—as long as your partner took good care of them, which they usually do, because they'd earned your trust in the first place. Your partners benefit from the business they didn't have to market for. And you benefit from the quid pro quo. As long as you choose partners whom you trust, you'll want to build partnerships whenever you can.

Features

Examples of features include podcasts, keynote opportunities, radio interviews, television interviews, and so on. In the five short years of my personal brand, I've been interviewed on global radio stations, television stations, and podcasts; I've given lectures on branding at universities; and I've given talks about the power of branding to audiences of up to 10,000 people. Many of these engagements I did for free. What these features typically expect from me is to that my tribe will pay attention to them; in return, they give me the chance to present my message at their campfires to their tribes. As a result, both our tribes march the access roads between our campfires and empires, creating an exchange of attention and viewership.

Many such engagements will include financial payment. But even those that don't involve remuneration do offer free publicity to feature your personal brand on as many distribution channels as you can leverage—social media and beyond.

If you're offered a feature, it's important that you assess the benefits you'll receive. If you're just starting out, you'll probably want to accept as many of these offers as possible. Once you're more established, you'll want to make sure that the opportunity will serve you in the long run. But in my experience they usually do. You can publicize what features you've done to highlight your personal brand and showcase that you are in demand, you're credible, and you're relevant. You can also use the opportunity to conduct other forms of business while you're in others' territory—sometimes taking advantage of free transportation and accommodation. At all such events you can promote everything you sell, and in particular whatever tangible products you sell—such as copies of books that you then autograph for each purchaser. (This opportunity to connect in person with strangers can be very beneficial.) In most cases the value you provide to others will come back to you and your tribe.

Don't underestimate the power of featuring yourself on as many channels as possible. Even without your own publicizing of these events, these features will validate that you do, in fact, know what you're talking about. In some instances, these long-term benefits can be priceless. The top five highest-paying clients I've ever done business with came to me because a feature event I accepted informed them of my existence. Feature opportunities are the reason I've been able to talk business with people from Citibank, Coca-Cola, Netflix, Pepsi, Red Bull, and more. I'm very grateful for all the opportunities I've been given, and I recommend you take advantage of everything you can.

Affiliates

Similar to sponsorships, affiliates are ongoing business between you and another entity. If your tribe ends up making a purchase via that link, you get a monetary kickback. This might sound like small potatoes, but the bigger your tribe becomes and the greater your influence to drive their attention, the more money you can make from affiliate relationships. These days, most established companies have an affiliate program with their marketing team whereby they actively seek influencers to conduct business with. If you have a tribe that shares interests and you can identify what they are, with a bit of prep work, you can set up your very own affiliation farm right next to your campfire and make money while you sleep.

We've done this with simple questions my tribe brings to me, such as, "Where do I get your equipment?" or "What books should I read to learn about branding?" For each product or service we simply approach the relevant retailers requesting an affiliate link, and then feature that link wherever it's appropriate. The best part is you don't need to be a big name to set up affiliate marketing programs for your personal brand. You just need to put in the legwork to set up your affiliate farm.

Access roads like these can open up a world of opportunities for you to import and export your goods. They can give you access to other tribes that you can absorb into your own (growing your brand more), enable business relationships you wouldn't have had otherwise, and enhance your image, credibility, and status in your industry and among your peers. Never underestimate the power of perception and reputation. Stoke the campfire and success will come.

The Rent-a-Tribe Effect

Picture this: you post on social media content of yourself on stage speaking to a live audience. What signal does that send to the rest of your audience? One of credibility and status. Remember, it's about perception.

The more of this status power you can build for yourself and your personal brand, the more you appear to be of value to anyone who looks at your profile. I call this the *rent-a-tribe effect*, and it's the biggest reward I've encountered. The more consistently you can stack this type of content, the more valuable you're perceived to be—a person of credibility and stature.

When you intentionally put yourself in situations where you can flex these opportunities to your tribe, you're communicating just that—credibility and status. When I started to input this sort of content into my feed—such as social validation through seeing me on podcasts, keynotes, stages, radio stations, television, and so on—I got texts, phone calls, and emails from friends congratulating me on all my success. The effect is the appearance of fame, the appearance of wealth, the appearance of being someone who's worthy of their tribe's money.

Networking

The third approach to capitalizing on success as an entrepreneur is the art of networking, which I still see as being at the heart of personal branding. Nothing is going to develop access roads between your campfire and other empires better and more effectively than the power of networking.

At the beginning of my personal branding journey, I took a hard look at my network. It was predominantly made up of local friends, colleagues, and associates I knew through other people. In analyzing this list more closely, I realized something that shocked me at first. Regardless of how much value I provided to those in my network—aside from my friends—nobody valued me more than they would complete strangers.

A mentor of mine once said, "Dain, your network will either help or hinder your ability to succeed in business." I thought about this a lot. The more I thought about it, the more it seemed that my network hindered me. Why? Because I was not providing value to this "tribe"—and had never really done so. My life at that time was pure survival, swinging from vine to vine, paycheck to paycheck.

So if I'd requested favors from my network then, most would have been reluctant to go out of their way to help me—whereas in my network now I'm surrounded by like-minded people, including people who operate on a level far beyond my own. Along my personal branding journey, I've studied what it truly means to succeed and what it truly means to build your own success, and I've identified what accounts for the difference between my network then and my network now. This massive change happened because I started to offer real value to my tribe. This, in turn, made it clear to other campfires that my value extended past my initial tribe, reaching far into a wider network that could get true value from me.

Networking, like building your tribe, is purely the raw exchange of value. What I'm talking about here is adding value to those around you in the real world, as well as people in the digital world. If you identify something that's important to someone you know, try to give it to them—without expecting anything in return. From my experience, people who are wealthy and successful reciprocate avidly. I've come to learn that people who are truly successful know this principle; they know why it's important to cultivate friendships and relationships in business, not just business deals. Their focus is on making things happen quickly and effectively. They know how important it is to establish access roads with others.

If you're looking to add gasoline to your campfire, start studying networking, and start paying close attention to how the players in business work together. To succeed as an entrepreneur is to constantly exchange value, to exchange imports and exports with as many people as possible as consistently as possible—in both the real world and the digital world.

The biggest mountain movers I've encountered have resulted from when I gave immense value to someone in my network who wanted to give back. It's honestly as simple as that. Grow your campfire while consistently providing value to others, and both avenues will feed each other.

Create a Pitch Deck

A simple tool I've exploited to fast-track networking is a personal branding pitch deck. Think of it as an ever-evolving promotional text and visual-based document that is the distillation of everything you do and all that you've achieved. As your personal brand grows and collects credibility and status, you'll want to update your pitch deck with the new details so you have them at the ready when opportunity calls.

My pitch deck includes the following:

- My brand story
- My tribe and what they care about

- Data and metrics on how much engagement I receive
- My focus on my five key themes and why I exist
- The problems I solve and how I solve them
- Credibility and accolades I've collected

And then, whenever we want to extend an invitation to create a new access road between myself and another campfire or empire, my marketing team simply sends this document.

We've created for you a pitch-deck template in multiple file formats for you that you can download for free to use for your personal brand. (See the end of this chapter for the scannable QR code. You're welcome.) Every time you accomplish something, add it to your pitch deck. As your personal brand grows, update your document.

And when you start building your access roads, just email your pitch to potential affiliates, partners, sponsors, networks, and features. Pair it with a short description that includes something like the following:

"Hey _____, I'm _____, and I'm hoping you could do me a massive favor. I'm looking to connect and find out how I can provide you with value at absolutely no cost. Please see the attached document that outlines how I can do this."

This may feel a little cringey, but I promise you it works. People are so curious on opening this email that they download the attached PDF just to see what's in it.

Just Fucking Decide

I've come to learn that building a network comes down to how much you become an initiator, a leader—and a self-promoter. Believe me, this will be uncomfortable for you at first, but it gets easier.

To be an initiator means that you decide. You don't wait. You promote. You don't wish, hope, and pray that opportunities come and find you—you go find them. In many cases, it's your job to build a road between yourself and an empire you wish to one day do business with, and as your campfire tribe grows, the greater the strike rate of landing these deals becomes. All you need to do to be an initiator is build your pitch deck and send it.

What I mean by being an initiator is you decide who your friends are, you decide who your sponsors are, and you decide who your partners are. And if you're going to be an initiator, why not initiate with the upper echelons of your industry?

And when you meet with them, consider doing what I do. When I'm engaging with my potential sponsors and partners, I repeatedly say, "We're friends." I say this when I really mean it, because I want to build genuine relationships. By just sending a pitch deck or introducing myself, half of the road between my campfire and their empire is already built. Telling them that I'm their friend plants the seed that they would perhaps like to reciprocate in some way. It's an authentic way to extend the hand of professional friendship to start a mutually beneficial relationship. Then, I stoke their appetite to *want* to build their half of our mutual access road by finding unique and interesting ways to provide them value, for free, at my expense, relentlessly—until they decide, "Alright, I'll build my half!" They then meet me halfway, and I keep my end of the bargain, successfully creating an access road between me and someone I wish to do business with.

In Conclusion

Access roads are game changers for your personal brand and how the public perceives you. Take advantage of these opportunities when they show up; from my experience, the more invitations you accept and then promote, the more invites and opportunities you'll receive.

Being conscious of leveraging these access roads is how my agency Rivyl lands big clients. It's how I've managed to spend evenings with celebrities such as Tom Brady, Tom Bilyiu, Seth Godin, Gary Vee, Lewis Howes, Jordan Belfort, and Simon Beard—still a bit amazed at how I got there.

I got there because I manufactured and engineered a perception of value around my personal brand. I got there by staying true to my initial 90-day brand plan and pivoting whenever necessary, and by leveraging all the relevant resources and opportunities that have come my way. And the entire time, I brought people along with me, creating mutually beneficial and cooperative campfires.

Access roads pave a path between you and other campfires so you can build more than just income—you can build lasting success and lasting relationships. If you take the time to carefully build this infrastructure, then you will progressively become less dependent on the social media algorithm (praise be the algorithm). Instead, you will become dependent on the relationships and networks you develop. This is a much more fruitful and sustainable way to grow your brand, because it's the relationships that I cultivated that have opened the biggest doors for me.

My tribe gained my personal brand weight, they gave my personal brand leverage. The greater my tribe, the greater my bartering chips, and the greater my access to people I can partner with. I've learned that in order to pave your path to the top, you need to invest considerable time in communication skills, negotiation skills, and relationship-building skills. And never forget that it's your tribe that will help you get there. Never take your tribe for granted—you always need to pay it back with more and more value every day and every way so you can get paid.

As I noted at the beginning of this book, I didn't start with any degrees. I didn't start with a perfect plan. I just started and went all out for 90 days. The momentum of my initial 90 days of learning how tribes think, and how to provide them with value and nurture them over the years, has meant I've been able to build Australia's fastest-growing brand agency, Rivyl.

Whatever your starting point is, start; whatever the deck of cards you've been dealt—deal them. This is what it takes for us entrepreneurs to succeed. We must execute consistently, and we must learn and develop a tribe who are holistically engaged. We must earn their trust, we must develop their appetite, and we must deliver on solving their problems to our utmost capacity. If you can do this, you can create an empire, one log at a time, one day at a time, one conversation at a time.

So make sure not to place any limits on yourself. Back yourself. Back your offering. And go out there and find out what works for you and what doesn't. To do that effectively, you'll need to apply a whole bunch of techniques and add even more specialties to your arsenal. I hope this book has provided that for you.

Exercise: Build Your Access Roads

A key ingredient of my success as a personal brand has been my constant pursuit of new and forever growing access roads, everything from sponsorships for equipment for my agency, partners to conduct and share business with, or podcast and speaking events to expand my tribe.

Access roads begin with you hunting for them; they don't always come to you. For me, this has been something I've constantly pursued.

The purpose of this exercise is for you to identify any and all potential access roads that exist around you, and how you can start building them between yourself and others. In the event, you don't have access roads—write down ones you wish to find, then go start building them for your personal brand.

Knowing the access road, and the first step, is half the battle. The second step is just starting the work: go make that phone call, send that email, shoot that text, book that coffee date.

Make access roads a constant priority; they require a bit of work to build, but once that highway is connected, it becomes easy to start conducting business with. The better connected you are, the more you'll attract new access roads to conduct business with.

List potential access roads:

-
-
-
-
-

-
-
-
-
-

List types of access roads:

(e.g., sponsorship, partnership, features, etc.)

-
-
-
-

-
-
-
-

What steps do I need to take to make this happen?

(e.g., send pitch deck to potential podcasts)

-
-
-
-

-
-
-
-

What impact would this have on my brand?

(e.g., expose my personal brand to new tribes)

-
-
-
-

-
-
-
-

Chapter Summary

This chapter focuses on leveraging all the learnings and success that come from sticking to the 90-day brand plant—the victories, the losses, the opportunities, and everything in between—all in service of creating what I call *access roads* to other campfires and villages. These access roads allow for easier exchanges of services and networking, including sponsorships, partnerships, features, affiliates, and more.

- **Sponsorships:** Growing tribes create growing influence. And combining your campfire or village with another means you have even more access to sponsorship opportunities. This also gives you organic credibility and relevance.
- **Partnerships:** These are opportunities to collaborate with other businesses or personal brands. You can export your tribe's influence and capabilities to them, and those businesses and personal brands can import theirs to you. This builds mutually beneficial relationships.
- **Features:** There are times when you can become a feature on other campfires, for example, podcasts, interviews, lectures, and so on. This is about creating more visibility and exposure for your personal brand.
- **Affiliates:** Affiliate relationships help create some form of passive income through access roads. You can earn commission from your tribe through services and products that you trust. This helps build credibility and forges bonds with other businesses or personal brands.

I also emphasize that by consistently showcasing your success and credibility on social media, you create what I call the *rent-a-tribe-effect*. This is essentially when your success draws in more tribe members. It's the best way to passively attract new people to your campfire or village. You can do this by creating a pitch deck and sending it to industry giants or anyone whom you want to work with. It's an invaluable tool in your 90-day brand plan.

Ultimately, my advice is to stick with the 90-day brand plan, learn quickly, and go out there and just start!

Free Chapter 11 Resources

I've designed a helpful guide to help you navigate this chapter's more in-depth and interactive secB tions. If you want to explore this in more detail, go to **dainwalker.com/resources/chpt11.** It's totally free, so make sure you don't miss out. You can also scan the QR code to get access.

Chapter 12

YOUR 90 DAY BRAND PLAN

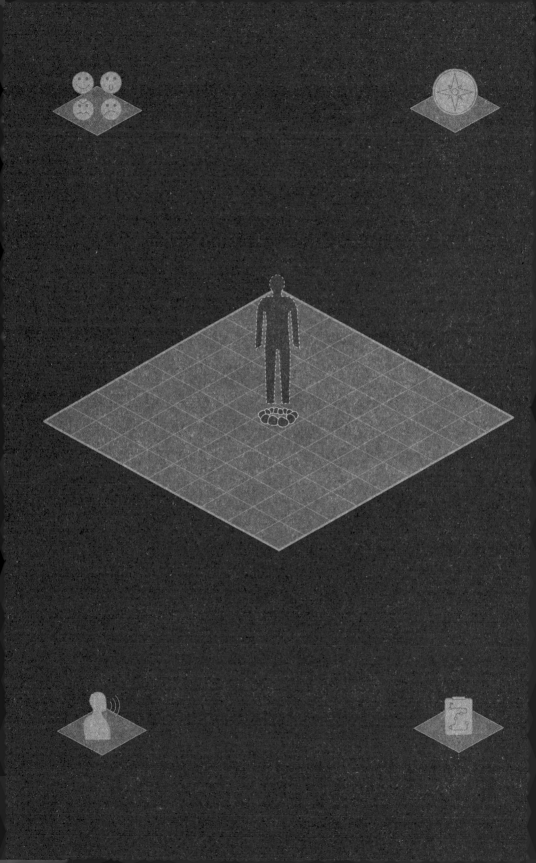

If you've made it this far into the book, you are likely in one of two situations:

- You've started your 90-day brand plan already. If so, congratulations. You're one of the few who have the courage to face your fear by deciding to start and amplify your very own campfire.
- You're yet to start and need that final nudge to kick things off.

In either case, I hope this summary gives you clarity and some things to focus on. Whatever the case, this is *your* 90-day brand plan, and it's your job to find your method.

My belief is that there is no right or wrong way to do this. I found my way, my clients have found theirs, and you need to find yours. This is a journey of self-expression, self-exploration, and self-amplification.

Self-expression: You need to get comfortable discovering how you will express yourself, how you will choose your five themes, how you will place your logs on the fire, and so on.

Self-exploration: You need to explore things you genuinely find interesting. That way, you'll never tire of exploring new and bigger ideas.

Self-amplification: You need to become comfortable with amplifying yourself to the world, to be in the public's eye, and to find ways to enjoy the process.

So, however you find your way, own it. It's yours. There are lessons to be learned everywhere, even from people who are in different fields from you. But my advice is that if someone has success with what you want to do (such as a big social following) take heed. They probably know something you don't.

How to Just Start

Alright, so if you need that final nudge to kick things off, this is my guide.

Post Content Every Day for 90 Days

Remember, your fire needs fuel daily to maximize the speed, growth, and trajectory of your tribe.

Tip: Actually produce the content each day, not in batches. You'll become a better creator because of it.

Make a Rule: For Each Day's Post, Reply to Every Comment You Get—on That Same Day

This is to boost the maximum possible engagement consistently.

Tip: If you reply to comments with questions, you'll get more comments.

Make a Rule: Respond Thoughtfully to Each DM You Get—on the Same Day You Get It

These small conversations and questions may feel like a chore at first, but these conversations turn into leads if you support and nourish them with thoughtful answers.

Tip: If you call people back and leave a voicemail, it will drastically increase your sales enquiries.

Start at Least One Access Road Every Single Day

Every day, find at least one person who has direct access to a network you want to get in front of and find ways to give them value. You don't have to know them. They may be strangers on the internet. Find out what they want less of in life, find out what they want more of in life—then creatively find ways to support them with your skills and talent.

Tip: If you become valuable to these people, they will become clients and your greatest asset for referrals.

Spend 15 Minutes Intensively Learning About Something Related to What Your Content Is About

Every day, invest at least 15 minutes of your time into learning something related to your field of expertise. It doesn't have to be about your topic of interest, but something at least that will enhance your ability to produce content, for example, camera presence, body language, effective communication, overcoming fear, and upskilling knowledge not just on your topic of interest but also all the things around it that can support you in becoming a better content creator, a better entertainer, or a better educator.

Tip: Fit these learnings in and around other things you're already doing, for example, getting dressed, eating, driving, exercising, organizing, chores, and so on. Also, a personal preference: I listen to podcasts at 1.5x speed to consume more content quicker.

Exercise Your Body Every Day

Every day, do something that puts your body under pressure. Not only is it good for your health but also the discipline required to show up and exercise is an important one for your mind. It gives you solitude to think, it kicks adrenaline into your veins, it releases dopamine and serotonin to put you in a good mood, and you'll feel 10x more confident and accomplished because of it. This is why I exercise in the morning, so throughout the day,

I already feel accomplished. Similar to a drug, I'm seeking the next hit from crushing an activity that's a part of my 90-day brand plan.

That being said, this was what helped me. What benefited me may be different for you, but I hope these examples serve as inspiration for you on how simple and how possible this all is when you break it down. What may exist as a giant monster in your head is just a menial task when applied to your calendar.

So as an example, here's a short summary of what a typical day of doing this looked like at the start of my 90-day brand plan. Keep in mind that this worked for me. It's likely yours is going to look different. So whatever the case, it's a good idea that you sit down after this and outline what your general day will look like, and always have some form of contingency plan in the event that something sporadic disrupts your day, such as, if I don't get my content done in the morning at 6 a.m., the alternative is that I'll do it at night at 9 p.m. The idea of laying out this schedule is to keep you accountable to yourself toward your goals and ambitions and to prioritize your time amplifiers over your time vampires.

 My First 90 Days Schedule

5:00 a.m.: Wake up, brush my teeth, and get into my gym clothes. (Note: I would not check my phone, I would be alone with my thoughts.)

5:15 a.m.: Listen to an audiobook about my industry while I make and eat breakfast.

5:40 a.m.: Drive to the gym—still listening to the audiobook.

6:00 a.m.: Exercise in the gym, listening to music. I need music, so I allow it here.

6:45 a.m.: Shower and dress for work.

7:10 a.m.: Drive to my (then) full-time job—still listening to the audiobook.

7:45 a.m.: Begin my workday.

11:45 a.m.: During my 30-minute lunch break I'd eat in the break room and write that day's content idea.

12:15 p.m.: Continue my workday.

5:00 p.m.: Drive home—still listening to the audiobook.

5:50 p.m.: Arrive home; debrief my day and connect with Elli.

6:20 p.m.: Cook dinner with Elli, discussing my idea for content that day.

6:35 p.m.: Eat dinner with Elli, spending quality couple time.

7:00 p.m.: Sit at my laptop and either produce a piece of graphic content or film myself on my iPhone making content.

8:00 p.m.: Spend 30 minutes replying to comments and DMs.

8:30 p.m.: Write captions and finalize hashtags for the new piece of content.

8:45 p.m.: Post the new piece of content.

8:50 p.m.: Reply to comments live as they show up on the feed.

9:00 p.m.: Reply to all comments on previous posts.

9:20 p.m.: Reply to all DMs with voice messages.

9:20 p.m.: Coordinate details of potential sales enquiries and book into my calendar.

9:30 p.m.: Write down my goals for the following day.

9:40 p.m.: Book any appointments, meetings, events, tasks, goals, and so on, into my calendar.

9:50 p.m.: Update and prepare my calendar for the following day.

10:00 p.m.: Shower and bed.

Now this calendar was my standard weekday during the very beginning when I had my full-time job. In the event you have more free time than this, great. I would invest as much additional time outside a schedule as I've outlined here into networking with like-minded people and booking consultation calls to prepare and offer your services. You can also work on developing your systems and product or service offerings.

At this time, however, when I had a full-time job, I would book such enquiries over the weekend and spend the majority of my Saturdays and Sundays discussing my services and pitching my offerings to potential prospects over Zoom calls. When closed, I would spend the remainder of my time on the weekends producing the deliverables for my clients.

I wanted to show you the typical schedule I had at the beginning of my journey, and as you can see, I had little time to invest as the majority of my time was invested in driving or working my full-time job. I want this to serve as a case that no matter how busy you are, you can make this plan work for you. As I stated at the beginning of this book, when executing this effectively, you may not have that job for long, or if you don't have a job, great, even better, even more argument that you should pour everything you have into getting yourself up and off the ground.

Remember, nobody is going to do this for you. Nobody can be motivated for you. It's not their job, nor others' responsibility to spoon-feed you through this process. If you want this to work, you have to want it. If you want this to succeed, you have to study relentlessly and actually become the type of person you need to become in order to become successful.

This is the moment that the rubber hits the road and your logs need to hit the fire. This is the moment you need to quit making excuses for why you haven't taken the plunge yet to get off your ass and make all of this work for you.

It's time for you to quit blaming everyone else around you, quit blaming your boss, quit blaming your spouse, quit blaming your lack of time, quit blaming your tiredness, quit blaming your lack of money, quit blaming how your parents raised you, quit blaming the area you grew up in, and quit blaming your lack of confidence or lack of attained skills.

There is but one person to blame, and that's you. You are single-handedly responsible for the life you're living right now. Once you accept that, you become invincible and you'll surely be monetized in the coming 90 days. Why? Because if the only thing you blame for the life you've created for yourself up and to this point is you, then you attain the power to change it. You become responsible for everything you have. And if you're responsible, guess who can change it? If you can create the current carnage that is your life, you can create the future bliss that your life could be.

Despite the fear, despite the risk, despite what people will think of you, just *start*. And if you can't do it for yourself, do it for your kids, do it for your partner, do it for your parents. All that lies between you and the beginning of the 90 days is a *decision*. If you can decide to start, and do it, you can have it.

So grab a shovel, dig a pit, light a fire, and start throwing logs in it.

Free Chapter 12 Resources

I've designed a helpful guide to help you navigate this chapter's more in-depth and interactive secB tions. If you want to explore this in more detail, go to **dainwalker.com/resources/chpt12**. It's totally free, so make sure you don't miss out. You can also scan the QR code to get access.

Notes

Chapter 1

1. Eamon Barrett, "When It Comes to Building Trust with Consumers, Brands Need to Put Customer Satisfaction First," *Fortune*, May 6, 2023, https://fortune.com/2023/05/05/when-it-comes-to-building-trust-with-consumers-brands-need-to-put-customer-satisfaction-first/.
2. Jane Solomon, "What Is an 'Influencer' and How Has This Word Changed?" Dictionary.com, January 7, 2019, https://www.dictionary.com/e/influencer/.
3. Kelly Phillips Era and Forbes Staff, "New Laws Threaten to Limit Foreign Ownership of Land Across the Nation," *Forbes*, November 2, 2023, https://www.forbes.com/sites/kellyphillipserb/2023/11/02/new-laws-threaten-to-limit-foreign-ownership-of-land-across-the-nation/?sh=15fc51375ef7.l.
4. *Harvard Business Review*, "Stop Screening Job Candidates' Social Media," September–October 2021, https://hbr.org/2021/09/stop-screening-job-candidates-social-media.
5. Jason Del Ray, "The Making of Amazon Prime, the Internet's Most Successful and Devastating Membership Program," *Vox*, May 3, 2019, https://www.vox.com/recode/2019/5/3/18511544/amazon-prime-oral-history-jeff-bezos-one-day-shipping.
6. Derek Blasberg, "How Jessica Alba Built a Billion-Dollar Business Empire," *Vanity Fair*, December 1, 2015, https://www.vanityfair.com/style/2015/11/jessica-alba-honest-company-business-empire.
7. Divya J. Shekhar, "Curiosity Will Teach You How to Build: Tony Fadell," *Forbes India*, June 5, 2023, https://www.forbesindia.com/article/leadership/curiosity-will-teach-you-how-to-build-tony-fadell/85373/1.
8. It's Nice That, "Under Construction: A Look Inside Walt Disney's Disneyland," September 3, 2018, https://www.itsnicethat.com/features/walt-disney-disneyland-taschen-publication-030918.

9. David Cassel, "Brendan Rich on Creating JavaScript in 10 Days, and What He'd Do Differently Today," The New Stack, August 26, 2018, https://thenewstack.io/brendan-eich-on-creating-javascript-in-10-days-and-what-hed-do-differently-today/.

10. Barbara Maranzani, "9 Things You May Not Know About the Pentagon," History.com, last updated May 5, 2023, https://www.history.com/news/9-things-you-may-not-know-about-the-pentagon.

11. Editors, "Sylvester Stallone Starts Filming *Rocky*," This Day in History [January 9, 1976], History.com, last updated January 7, 2020, https://www.history.com/this-day-in-history/stallone-starts-filming-rocky.

12. Meg Matthias/The Editors of *Encyclopaedia Britannica*, "Hundred Days," last updated October 27, 2023, Britannica, https://www.britannica.com/event/Hundred-Days-French-history.

13. Drew Hendricks, "How the 25 Richest Americans Failed Miserably," *Inc. Australia*, July 15, 2014, https://www.inc-aus.com/drew-hendricks/how-the-top-25-richest-americans-failed-before-during-or-after-they-made-million.html.

Chapter 2

1. https://dictionary.cambridge.org/dictionary/english/impostor-syndrome.

Chapter 8

1. Plain Language.gov, "Federal Plain Language Guidelines," last revised May 2011, https://www.plainlanguage.gov/guidelines/.

Appendix

FAQs

Q: **Should I rush to monetize the first lucrative idea I have?**

A: Too many people monetize their initial ideas, which they've cooked up without much thought. They sprinkle some entrees and serve them to their tribe, then come to realize the way they want to position themselves, their offer, and their set of deliverables way too late. Your cooking will inevitably continue to evolve over time, and you need to account for that pivot.

Q: **Why do you call your personal brand a campfire?**

A: The idea of the campfire is to provide heat and a place for your tribe to spend their time. Eventually, when you foster enough heat, a tribe begins to form, and that tribe will grow a connection with you and your brand to the point where a portion of them will begin to be hungrier for more than just the warmth of your fire. More content. More offerings. More tiers of service.

Q: **Will I see immediate monetary gains?**

A: The simple answer is no. Personal brand is a journey with many aspects that you need to consider. And all of this has to be done the right way. Monetizing yourself and your brand will take time. It's a slow burn. First, you need to learn how to cook. Mastering content creation is one component, building a relationship with your community is another, and the third is learning to monetize everything you've created without angering or alienating your tribe.

Q: **Where should I even begin my personal branding journey?**

A: The best place to start is exactly where you are right now. The only thing holding you back from embarking on your journey is you.

191

Remember that no one else has the keys to your success. No one else can do it for you. Begin by finding your niche—that being the one thing that you're really passionate about. Don't focus on being clever at this stage; just focus on identifying your niche and be clear at all times. Be clear about what you can offer and how you can offer it. Start by visualizing your future self and ask yourself what that would look, sound, and feel like. Then you can start to think about the type of tribe you'd like to attract. At the end of the day, you need to just start without letting yourself fall into self-doubt. Just go for it. You won't regret it.

Q: **How do I develop my personal brand values?**

A: This comes about once you've identified your niche. For example, if your niche is in the mindset coach space, then your personal brand values will be based on growth and adaptability. Pick one angle that comes from this and begin to jot down any ideas that come to you, keeping in mind that you always need to provide value and give actionable insights. If you're a musician, then discipline and repetition could be part of your values. Stay vigilant and keep auditing your values to ensure that you're serving your potential tribe.

Q: **What do I do if I don't get the engagement I expect?**

A: Don't worry about that in the beginning. First, focus on creating entertaining and engaging content, then you can focus on how it's received. If, after a long while, you don't see much engagement, then you need to audit your content and the way you're showcasing it. Take stock of your place in the market and how you can make yourself known more. If you're still struggling, it might be time to pivot your niche. At the end of the day, the most important thing you need to account for is the attention and engagement of your tribe. Be valuable to them, and, in time, you will get the engagement you're looking for.

Q: **I'm struggling to monetize my content. What should I do?**

A: This could be because of a few things. You might be too early in your process, or you haven't effectively identified exactly what it is that your tribe is willing to pay for. Always keep in mind that the majority of your tribe will not have the purchasing power to give you an intense return on investment (ROI). If you know that you're catering to your tribe's desires, then stay vigilant and keep on working toward making your content and services more accessible and consistently easy to understand and grasp.

Q: **I'm scared to change my product offerings. What do I do?**

A: This is something you'll honestly just have to get over. If you're looking to truly offer authentic value to your tribe, you have to be willing to pivot to give them exactly what they need. Don't be precious about your product suite. Constantly audit it and stay adaptable to changes in your market's landscape. Be ready to change, and embrace the power of flexibility. It's the only way to ensure that you don't get left behind in the competitive market of personal branding.

Q: **What if I'm scared to be on camera or talk in front of people?**

A: Believe it or not, I had the exact same fear. I wasn't comfortable talking on camera, let alone in front of a massive crowd. The answer may not be what you're hoping for, but this will honestly get better through exposure. You have to put yourself in situations where speaking in front of people or on camera becomes a necessity. Something you can't run away from. That's what I did. I've even spoken to crowds of up to 10,000 people! Even I'm surprised at how much I've grown in this space, but with enough tenacity and exposure, so will you.

Q: **How do I deal with imposter syndrome and self-doubt?**

A: This is something that you might have to manage for as long as you wish to pursue, grow, and evolve your personal brand. Even with all my experience and validation from external sources, I still feel a sense of self-doubt and like a bit of an imposter when I attend large events or get praise from industry giants. It's a fleeting feeling, but it still happens from time to time. It's totally natural; don't beat yourself up about it. Accept that it's part of the journey, and even take some positives away from it. Feeling this way shows that you're constantly auditing yourself. Just back yourself, trust your process, and keep going. If your tribe likes what you're doing, then don't listen to that negative inner voice.

Index